100 Effective ways *for* Self DEVELOPMENT

J.M. Mehta

PUSTAK MAHAL®

Publishers
Pustak Mahal

Administrative office and sale centre
J-3/16 , Daryaganj, New Delhi-110002
☎ 011-23276539, 23272783, 23272784, 23260518
E-mail: info@pustakmahal.com • *Website:* www.pustakmahal.com

Branches
Bengaluru: ☎ 080-22234025, 40912845
E-mail: pustakmahalblr@gmail.com
Mumbai: ☎ 022-22010941, 22053387
E-mail: unicornbooksmumbai@gmail.com

ISBN 978-81-223-1418-2

Edition: 2021

Printed at : Glorious Printers, Delhi

Preface

A disciple asked a holy man, who was his Guru – "What is the purpose of life?" The guru gave a cryptic reply – "The purpose of life is, a life with a purpose". The answer was hidden in the question itself. But another question props up – 'What is that purpose?' To my mind, that purpose is self-development. In other words, we can make our life purposeful through self-development.

In order to make our life purposeful, the process of self-development has to be undertaken at all levels which include physical, mental, emotional, moral, economic, social and spiritual. The development has to be all round, not lopsided. The process of self-development starts right from birth till end. A newly born baby develops into a walking-talking toddler, a bubbling youth and an adult with the passage of time. Development is a natural process, but much effort has to be made to achieve perfection.

In order to attain self-development, one has to find appropriate ways and means and put them into practice. Mere knowledge is not enough unless it is put into practice. There is a popular saying 'Practice makes a man perfect.' This small book is an attempt to tell the reader some very effective ways and means for self-development. We call these means 'RECIPES' in order to make the serious subject tasty and easily acceptable, just as we have recipes for useful medicines and dainty dishes.

It is hoped that the readers will enjoy these recipes and actually implement them in order to make their lives worthy and purposeful.

— J.M. MEHTA

Contents

1. Human Life

This is the most precious and priceless gift of God to mankind. There is no possession, property or prize superior to human life. Man is on top of creation.

There is no physical body, equal in worth or better than human body, in its normal, natural, healthy state. Each organ given to man is unique in nature and priceless in value. Human intelligence is far superior to that of any other species. One can produce or process most material things through human life but all natural things combined cannot create human life. In conclusion, the value and importance of human life can never be over-estimated.

If such is the importance and value of human life, it becomes most essential to think and plan how it should be lived. In short it should be lived in a proper, planned and developed manner based on certain well-thought values, principles and acts. A human being is not born just to eat drink and procreate, just like an animal does. He is endowed with a wonderful body, senses, mind and intelligence. These assets must be developed and utilized in a purposeful, peaceful and progressive manner. Human life provides a golden opportunity which must not be wasted in wild pursuits and negative hungry action.

2. Know the Purpose of Life

Most human beings live life aimlessly in a mechanical way – Just for survival .We often move like a feather that moves with the wind. In this manner, human life becomes chaotic and follows a confused lifestyle without any proper direction. We find ourselves lost and entangled in the worldly web. This is not a proper scenario of human life.

What is then the purpose of human life? Someone has said 'The purpose of life is – LIFE WITH A PURPOSE'. But we often confuse PURPOSE with profession or career or some material objective which is important to us at a particular stage of time. Thus different things at different time become ones main purpose of life. Sometimes it is money or material possessions, fame and power, job and career prospects or some other enjoyments and acquisitions. But all these things cover only one aspect.

Living life for mere existence is not enough. Human life has a vast field for interplay and action. Giving life a purpose is giving direction to life to reach a destination. When one knows the purpose of life, one works for it. Thus by fulfilment of that purpose and by reaching the desired destination, one gets satisfaction that leads to happiness.

The fundamental purpose of life should be progress and development in all spheres which include physical, mental, social and spiritual. One should work for success in all these four directions. Reaching the full purpose of life is a difficult task. One has to put body, mind and soul in constant effort to reach the goal. In short, the purpose of life is self-development.

3. Life Has many Shades

It is said 'Change is the law of nature.' It is so with human life which is never the same always. It is ever changing and has a lot of variety. Life is like a journey with numerous stops and stages. Thus changing, it moves on from one stage to another, from one shade to another, from one scene to another and so on.

Let us look at the process of life from birth to death. A crying infant grows into a bubbling baby. Soon the toddler transforms into a walking-talking and running young lad. Childhood enters youth, goes on to middle age followed by decline and death. In this life long process one passes through different shades, experiences and happenings. Pleasure and pain, joy and sorrow, gain and loss, ups and down keep on recurring.

Life keeps on changing and there is nothing everlasting. We must draw a useful conclusion from changing aspects of life. We should always keep in mind that change is the recurring feature of life. Every stage passes away and nothing is permanent. Such an attitude towards different happenings in life should produce a spirit of detachment. We should take all these changes in a calm manner and never lose heart and grumble in vain. We should always trust life and remember the following advice.

"Life is great for those who appreciate it, difficult for those who worry about it, and terrible for those who always complain and criticise."

4. *Live Like Lotus*

Lotus is the national flower of India.

Its significance has been described in ancient Indian holy scriptures. Lotus has been mentioned with reverence in Buddhist, Confucius and Taoists philosophies. Its beauty and purity has inspired many poets, artists, writers and thinkers as well. The lotus posture of Lord Buddha and Mahavira draws universal admiration and respect.

The lotus state of meditation has mystically led many saints and devotees to self-realization. The peculiarity of lotus is that in spite of its growth in muddy water, it remains untouched by water and unpolluted by filth. It teaches us a moral and spiritual lesson. One who lives in this world which is polluted by evil, but performs duty without attachment and concern for fruits, remains unaffected by sin. Despite its roots in mud, the lotus flower remains above the mud, untouched by dirty water below. It ascends upward towards sunshine, from the darkness beneath.

In Buddhist philosophy, lotus signifies the state of awakening of the purity of soul which is free from sinful desires and actions. Thus lotus acts as a symbol of inspiration to make our life pure. Just as lotus ascends above the mud in the filthy water of the pond, in the same way, we should keep our mind and soul away from the dirt of material desires, sins and sorrows of the mundane life.

Living life like lotus can lead to enlightenment that will liberate us from the sufferings of existence and bring us the bliss of liberation.

5. *Live in the Present*

TIME has three dimensions – *past, present and future*. Of these, PRESENT is the most important and valuable. In fact the other two evolve out of what is present. It was once the present which rolled into past and the future also becomes present with the passage of time.

The real advantage of life lies in its living in the present. The secret of success in life is based on the fact that one should seize the present and make the best use of it. In order to expect a better future, one should utilise its present in the best possible manner.

It is no use brooding or grumbling about past mistakes and happenings and the uncertainties of the future which is beyond us. This is a bad habit that must be discarded forthwith. We should learn from our mistakes and should never repeat them. If we take care of our present, the future will take care of itself. An opportunity missed is opportunity lost. It is observed that life seldom gives the same chances again. Therefore one should seize the present moment and act accordingly.

It is of great advantage to do eight things at the right time and the best time to do is now, the present time. We should never allow it to slip away and then repent. A good opportunity knocks at the door once. Either you make use of it or let it go. The choice lies with you. Always keep in mind the following couplet:-

Past is history
Future is mystery
Time now is a gift
We call it PRESENT

In conclusion, learn to live in the present and make the best use of it.

6. Respect Time

What is human life?

It is just Time stored in moments, days, months and years. Our life is counted by the yardstick of time. It is the time span between birth and death which makes life. Time, therefore, is utmost important and we must give it due respect and not waste it.

Time has dynamic nature. It never stops, goes on and passes away. It is movement which is ever flowing and is never the same like the flowing water in a river. The time which has passed away never comes back. The following brief description of time is indicative of its fleeting and precious nature:

Time flies, it marches on
Time and tide wait for none
Catch time by the forelock
Time is money, time is life.

As time is a precious commodity, it should never be wasted. It should be used properly, wisely and for the general good. Benjamin Frankilin, a great thinker said about time as follows:

"If you love life, then do not squander time, for that is the stuff life is made of."

Time should not be wasted in useless and wild pursuits. It is not good to remain idle as an idle mind is devils workshop. One should always remain involved in a useful activity. In view of the dynamic nature of time, it is always fleeting. There is never enough time to do all the things one wants to do. Therefore, do your best to do as much useful and constructive work as you can do in the available time.

All time should be planned properly and suitable space should be provided to various chores of daily life. Thus there should be time for work, to exercise, to read and relax, to meet people, to sleep, to meditate, to serve others, etc. There should always be time for leisure, pleasure, entertainment, play, etc.

In short, we should respect time and use it for our good and for the welfare of others, as well.

7. Be Good and Do Good

The gist of ancient Indian philosophy may be concluded in one sentence – 'Be good and do good.' Our scriptures teach us to lead a pure, pious and peaceful life, based on basic principles of love, truth, non-violence, justice etc. All other good qualities of head and heart evolve from these fundamentals.

The means to adopt and practice this noble doctrine lies in requiring good qualities. If we have good qualities we shall be good and do good deeds. There is a saying 'Do unto others, as you would have them do to you'. We definitely expect goodness from others. It, therefore, becomes incumbent upon us to be good to others.

It may not be too difficult to do good to others sometime but it is much more difficult to be good. To be good, one has to do good always. When you start doing good, doors keep opening for doing more good. One good deed may lead to more. The great CHANAKYA says: 'The fragrance of flowers may spread only in the direction of the wind, but the goodness of a person spreads in all directions'.

A good person is the best friend as he cannot do you any harm and will always try to help you. He is trustworthy, honest, reliable and will never deceive you. One must therefore cultivate friendship with good persons and also be friendly to others, as far as practicable.

The path of goodness is not easy. Anyone who proposes to be good may not expect people to roll out red carpets for him. Instead he may have to face brickbats sometime. But one must traverse the path of goodness with patience, perseverance, determination and goodwill for others.

8. Never Give Up

Life is not a bed of roses, there are thorns attached to flowers as well. Life does not offer a straight path. It is full of turns, ups and downs, rough and tough ways. There are obstacles on the way, big or small. One feels happy in favourable circumstances. But what should we do when the path is not straight and smooth, easy and comfortable. Do we turn back and stop our journey if there is a huge boulder or a big tree fallen on the road? If we cannot remove it, we chalk out an alternative route to reach our destination.

In the life long journey, ups and downs are part and parcel of human life. Disappointments, depression, problems and failures, differences and difficulties are bound to arise in life. These changes and obstacles should make life more meaningful and strong. In the battle, the brave do not run away from the battle field. They face hunger and thirst, fire and battles but keep on marching ahead and cross all hurdles to win the battle. Problems can be faced with patience and perseverance while turbulences should produce tolerance and tactfulness. The difficulties of life are the means to make it more resilient, realistic and reliable.

We should learn lessons of perseverance, endurance and hard work from ants and small birds and small children who keep on struggling against difficult situations. An ant carries a burden of more than its body weight. A tiny tot gets up ever after falling down many times. Small birds build their nests facing all odds. Think of the hardship faced by soldiers in the battlefield, farmers in their crop fields, mountaineers while climbing and so on. The motto of life should be "Never give up". Keep on marching forward towards your destination.

9. Mind Your Mind

Mind is the fulcrum around which human life revolves. It is the mind that thinks, imagines, plans, resolves and thus plays a very vital role in the mind-body-soul setup. Our worldly life is an interplay of success, mind and intelligence etc. The soul provides the basic energy for the functioning of the mind and its associates.

The GITA points out the high status of the mind in human life, in the following verse:-

'The senses are great, greater than the senses is the mind, but greater than the mind, is the intelligence....'

Thus the mind occupies a place above the senses. There are five sources of knowledge and four sources of action. The mind acts as a coordinator between them. When the mind comes under the influences of the senses, it gets deluded and becomes a slave of the senses. When it runs after the senses, the understanding gets distorted. Consequently, attachment and anger are produced leading to bewilderment, loss of memory, intelligence and total ruin. It is therefore utmost essential to keep the mind under proper control.

The nature of mind is restlessness. It is ever changing and fast moving. It is the fastest moving entity, faster than sound and light. Therefore, it is extremely difficult to control it. But it is possible to do so through the constant practice of non-attachment over a long period. It requires lot of patience, perseverance and yogic discipline.

Thoughts, ideas and images flow though mind endlessly. Sense perceptions clutter over mind with the images of the external world and past experiences and happenings. This state of flux of mind leads to worries, depression, fears, anxiety, confusion and the consequent suffering. It is therefore essential to exercise control which can bring inner peace and remove suffering and bring happiness.

There are different ways to control the mind. A common way is to let thoughts flow freely and just be a witness to their thoughts. Another way is to remember God and to dwell in His thoughts. One may recite ones favourite mantra and practice the belief that mind is your slave and you are its master.

Regular practice of PRAANAYAAM is a healthy exercise to control the mind. This method brings stillness that puts a proper check on the mind and thus guides it to the right path of restraint and rectitude. In Verse 35 of CHAPTER VI, THE GITA tells us the ultimate method to control the mind, as follows:

"Without doubt, the mind is difficult to restrain, but it can be controlled by constant practice and non-attachment."

The GITA shows the way to mind our mind. Let us follow it for our peace, progress and self-development.

10. *Be Honest*

HONESTY is one of the best virtues of a human being. First of all, we should be honest with ourselves before we are honest with other members of our society. It means we should do what we say.

A philosopher has said, "Honesty is much more than not lying. It is truth telling, truth speaking, truth loving and truth living." Thus truth is the very basis of honesty. Without truth there can be no honesty. These are the two sides of the same coin.

An honest person, primarily has to be a person who loves truth and lives by truth. He is fair and straight forward in his dealings with others. He is without any greed and is free from deception. Honesty makes him capable of love, kindness, and compassion. An honest person may have to face problems and suffering in the material world. He may become a victim of jealousy, anger and ridicule of dishonest people around him. But he can face all these hardships with his inner strength, determination and inspiration of his convections.

Sometimes he may have to withstand false allegations but he will stand as a rock and counter falsehood. The power of honesty is greater than any other material power and that leads to inner calm, moral strength, peace of mind and enduring happiness.

It is said, 'Honesty is the best policy'. So we should try to be honest in all circumstances in spite of all odds that may arise in this process. In the final stage it will pay rich dividend. Being honest in itself is a great virtue and has its own reward.

11. *Pray for Peace and Progress*

'More things are wrought by prayer than this world dreams of' **Alfred Tennyson**

People pray to God on account of variety of reasons. Generally they pray for health, wealth and happiness. Most people pray for wealth and well-being and progeny. Some pray for success in some venture, for status and power in society. Many people pray while in some distress, disease or some other type of suffering.

Some pray out of fear of God who is almighty and all powerful. There are others who pray as a matter of duty, daily routine or as a religious ritual. Some pray out of compulsion as instructed by parents or a guru.

But there is a special category of people who pray with deep devotion, love and utmost reverence for God, in a spirit of self-surrender and all humility. This is the best form of prayer as prayer should arise out of deep faith in God, otherwise it will be meaningless.

There are various methods of prayer. Some pray before an idol, some before a holy book and some perform *havan* and recite holy mantras. Some perform worship before the sun, the moon, at a holy place, beside a river or on top of a hill or in a place of worship etc.

An easy and effective method to pray is to pray in SILENCE, at a solitary place free from, noise and disturbances and without asking for any material benefit and worldly pleasures, etc. Such a prayer is for peace, progress and development.

12. Remember God Always

God is our creator. It is, therefore utmost important to maintain close link with God. How can we do it? God is formless and invisible. We can establish link with HIM by remembering HIM, as far as possible. In order to cultivate this habit of remembering God, we must have full faith in HIM.

First of all, we should be aware that all this creation owes its existence to God. We should also be aware of his various attributes, powers and functioning. In order to have a close link with God, it is very important to inculcate the habit of remembering HIM right from childhood. Parents have to play a proper role in this direction. This passion should grow more and more with the passage of time. As one enters youth, one should start practicing meditation. As this practice continues over a long period, the thought and remembrance of GOD will become well entrenched in the mind. As one grows in age and experience this habit will grow into a passion and one will remember god always while walking or doing anything else.

In order to progress in life and to gain success one needs some outside support besides one's own efforts. Thus we need support of our parents, teachers, friends, relatives and companions etc. Besides these avenues of help, we need inspiration and support of the Supreme Power, we call GOD. His support and inspiration will be forthcoming if we remember HIM at all times or as far as possible.

Remembrance of God enables us to lead an honest life based on moral values. Simplicity, humility, devotion, total surrender are the main means to support of God. Constant remembrance of God throughout our life, with full devotion will create noble virtues in us and thus will make our life happy and peaceful.

13. *Have Confidence in You*

In order to attain success in life, it is very important to have self-confidence. It is necessary to cultivate will power and determination to gain self-confidence. A human being is endowed with the capacity and capability to do many things. Therefore there should be no lack of self-confidence.

In order to build up self-confidence, one should first try to practice with small things as it is easy to attain success in these things. As one learns to do small things, small job, one gradually gains confidence to do more difficult things. In this way one can increase both strength and stamina to do bigger jobs. Take the example of a toddler who first crawls, then learns to stand and thereafter starts walking and running. In the same way success in solving small problems leads you to have more confidence to surmount bigger problems.

However, there is a word of caution! One need not be over-confident. First of all you must try to know the nature and the extent of any work or problem you face and then try to work out ways and means to do it. You have to first equip yourself with necessary means to do what you have to do. It may be harmful to attempt what may be beyond your known capacity and capability. In such situations, you will have to seek help and co-operation of others.

Life is full of problems and difficulties at all stages. One needs self-confidence to face all odds, besides other aids. It is only then that success may be achieved. The motto should be 'Yes, I can do it' and then find ways and means to do it.

Remember the saying 'Try, Try again boys, you will succeed at last'. Therefore, maintain the spirit of self-confidence always.

14. Keep Fit and Fine

"Health is the Greatest Wealth." **(Mahabharata)**

Health is the greatest asset to live life well. It is, therefore, our first and foremost duty to keep ourselves fit and fine. Good health is a priceless possession and a valuable aid for a human being. It is most essential for happy living, progress and prosperity. It is more useful than any other acquisition of material life.

Health is essential to enjoy the benefits of wealth. A healthy person can earn wealth but an ailing wealthy person longs for health. His wealth is not of much use, if he does not enjoy good health. The importance of good health cannot be overestimated. One must, therefore, make all efforts to be fit and fine.

Proper food, regular exercise, practice of brahmacharya, good thoughts, good company, desirable habits, proper rest and recreation are some of the most important means to keep good health. A smile, moderate, healthy lifestyle is beneficial in maintaining good health. All sorts of addictions which include smoking, drinking, drugs etc. must be avoided. Vegetarian diet which includes seasonal fruits and vegetables, milk products etc are generally recommended to keep healthy.

In view of the great importance of good health, one must make all efforts and take suitable precautions to keep fit and fine. Parents have a vital role to play to keep their wards in good health right from their birth. An early education and training will enable children to keep good health in later life.

15. *Limit Your Desires*

Desires act as a catalytic agent for actions in life. There is hardly anyone who is free from desires. The pursuit and fulfillment of desirable desires can lead to success, progress and happiness in life.

A desire is a passionate feeling born out of attraction and attachment to an object. Desires in some shape and form are always being produced in the mind of an individual. If one desire is fulfilled, another crops up or the urge to fulfill some other desire arises again and again. It is generally observed that desires are never satiated. Desires are useful in some way but their unlimited play can lead to destruction. Lord Buddha said "Desire is the cause of all misery." He further said that "The causes of suffering is nothing but selfish desires." It is therefore, almost essential to keep a proper control over all desires.

The best way to deal with desires is to restrict them in daily life to the level of necessities. One has to fulfil these desires as a matter of duty. However the field of desires should not be expanded. As a general rule, all unnecessary cravings must be curbed. All genuine needs should be satisfied but desires must not become needs. One should therefore maintain a proper control over desires rather than satisfy these without any limit. At the same time, desires cannot be suppressed completely. The solution lies in the right reasoning and proper understanding of the consequences of fulfillment of desires. Strong determination on the repeated reminders are helpful in curbing unnecessary harmful desires. Desires should be kept within limit and under control from the very beginning and this practice should be continued throughout life.

16. *Work is Worship*

Most people worship God by mere words, reciting some mantra or bowing their heads before a statue or a holy book or in some other way but they do not perform good deeds. Such worship is false and of no avail. God does not need our prayer or any form of ritual worship.

True worship lies in the performance of noble deeds such as charity, spread of true knowledge, removal, of ignorance and evils and helping the poor and the deserving needy people, in whatever way possible. Service of mankind is the service of God.

The VEDA says, 'Worship God with your deed and not by words alone'. God expects us to be good, honest, noble and pure. The human beings have to do some duty and perform some work in different ways. One should perform one's duty or perform work honesty and to the best of one's capacity, with a good intention and purpose. This is the best form of worship.

All work should be performed in the spirit of dedication to the word. Whether it is walking, clearing, cooking, eating or any other professional work it should be done for the sake of God with true devotion. In this way we will do the work in the best possible manner. If we perform each action of our daily life throughout life, such work will become worship in true spirit of complete surrender. All work performed in this manner will justify the saying 'Work is worship'.

17. *Say Good Bye to Worries*

A common saying says, 'Don't worry, Be happy'. It means that in order to be happy, one should not worry. However in real life there is hardly anyone who is free from worries which are many and of different nature. We worry for our family, career, finances and so on.

In general we worry about our deficiencies and draw-backs, needs and desires, relation with others, disease and death etc. Then we have fears that worry us. We worry about problems being faced by us in our daily life. At the same time we worry about our future also. We also worry about what is happening in our society, country and the world also. Thus we have a bag full of worries and this is not a happy state. We should, therefore, find out a way to be free from worries.

First of all we should try to know the cause of any worry. Once we know the cause, it may not be difficult to find a solution. If we suffer from a disease we should consult a doctor. Similarly other problems which are causing worry must be sorted out after knowing the cause of these problems. The cause of worry should never be ignored or left unattended. Nip the evil in the bud. One should not run away from the problem but face it bravely and remove the hurdle.

In order to remove worries one can also take help from others. If no help is forthcoming then try your best and leave the rest to God. But remember God helps those who help themselves and are fully devoted to HIM. First deserve before you desire. In this manner one can say good bye to worries and be happy.

18. Do not Grieve

THOMAS HARDY, the great English novelist said, 'LIFE is a general drama of pain with an episode of happiness here and there in between'. For a large number of people, life is like that. Their life is full of grief for various reasons. There is shortage of wealth, some suffer from a disease, there are others who are left without any child, some are jobless and cannot make both ends meet. Many people suffer because of ill-treatment of others in society. There are multitude of people suffering from poverty, the under privileged, the disabled and the downtrodden who are victims of great grief. You ask anyone on the roadside or in your neighbourhood and he will tell you some story on his grief. Then there is mother of all grief – the death. In short, most people grieve due to some cause. Now how to deal with such situation?

The GITA shows the ways, as mentioned in the following verse:-

'Wise men do not grieve for the dead or for the alive'. The incidence of grief happens due to unfavourable situations. It may be due to disease, deficiency, failure, defeat and dishonour. One must understand the fact that grieving, weeping or complaining will not help. That will make the problem worse. Therefore, do not grieve. Face your problems with courage and determination. Have faith in God and in your efforts and do your best. Try to remain upbeat and do not dishearten. Have positive approach and hope for the best. Remember, the famous lines of Shelley, the English poet, who said, *'If winter comes can spring be far behind'*. In this way, you can surmount your grief and make your life worth living.

19. Pleasure of Reading

Good literature forms the foundation of the wisdom and one can acquire that wisdom through reading. Alexander Pushkin, the world renowned Russian writer has said about reading as follows:-

'READING is the BEST LEARNING. To follow a great man's thought is the most entertaining of the science.'

Reading is to the mind, what physical exercise is to the body. Mind is the fulcrum around which all activities of the body rotate. As physical exercise keep the body healthy, moving and in good shape, in the same way mental exercise through good reading keep the mind active, healthy and positive.

Reading of good literature has several advantages. First of all it provides information that is useful for human life. Then it is a source of knowledge about persons, places, arts, science, history, geography, health, diseases, careers and so many other things. Besides it is a good source of entertainment and relaxation which are necessary for good life.

It is through reading that we meet great people and prophets, saints and philosophers etc. By knowing their thought and philosophy we can improve our thought and character. Reading of great epics like *Ramayana* and *Mahabharata* can act as a great source of wisdom. Reading of books on poetry, humour etc. gives us great pleasure and pleasant thoughts. Books on religion and spirituality teach as moral values upon which we can build our whole personality and lead a worthy life.

Thus reading can bring multifarious benefits to improve our life and for self-development as we spend our time in useful and positive manner. Therefore, cultivate the habit of good reading from the very beginning.

20. Try to Remain Content

Contentment is the greatest wealth. **[Mahabharata]**

Contentment is the key to a peaceful and happy life. A content person does not run after making more and more money, acquiring fame and power etc. He is therefore not adversely affected in the absence of these acquisitions.

In order to remain content, we should first try to understand its meaning and implications. It implies the absence of desire to possess more of the necessities of life than are really needed for its proper maintenance. It further implies that in normal life, one should work honestly to one's full capacity and be satisfied with what one gets. There should be no complaint, regret or repentance. It is a calm state of mind with inner mental poise that does not depend upon external influences and circumstances.

Contentment however, does not mean passivity, laziness or lack of action. It does not mean that one should do nothing to achieve progress in life or withdraw herself from home or society and become a recluse. Of course, one should try to make all possible efforts for self-development and progress in life. These should be no anger, greed or grumblings, if one does not get what one wants, even after making all efforts. In order to reach this state, one has to develop an attitude of contentment on gradual and continuous basis as it does not evolve all of a sudden. Patience, perseverance, tolerance and right understanding are necessary means to attain contentment.

In short, contentment is the glad acceptance of what comes to you by providence or circumstance after making best efforts. It brings cheerfulness, peace, purity, balance of mind and moral strength to face all ups and downs of life. Therefore, practice contentment and be happy.

21. Celebrate your Marriage

Man and woman are made for each other. They are also complimentary to each other. Either is incomplete without the other. Marriage is, therefore an essential event of life to come together, to love together. It should be celebrated in the best possible manner with mutual consent. In the long run, marriage should be your key to long life and happiness.

In Indian culture and tradition, marriage is a life-long partnership between two like-minded individuals by mutual consent. The ideal marriage is with the consent of two celebate persons who have acquired knowledge, righteousness and good health. There should be similarity of views, temperaments and character. Prior to the fixation of marriage, the two should have ample opportunity to converse with each other, to know each others' views and habits, under the patronage of their parents. In such cases of loving and enlightened relationship, there is no question of divorce after marriage.

Marriage is a bond of life long companionship between two partners, on the basis of equality and mutual respect. Secondly, this bond has to be utilised for producing progeny, for the promotion of human race and for family life. It may also be considered as a proper means for the satisfaction of natural sexual instinct in a beneficial well-regulated manner. However, marriage is not an open license merely for sexual gratification.

Someone said 'Marriage is an edifice that must be rebuilt every day.' The success in marriage is more than finding the right person. It is a matter of being the right person. Besides being the union of the bodies, it is also the alliance of the two minds and the souls. Therefore love and celebrate your marriage in the right way.

22. Keep Smiling

Shakespeare said *'Smile is sunshine in a home.'*

A smile can act as a barometer for your emotions; it can also be an ornament or a mask on your face. A smile is such a wonderful tool that you can break ice with it. Remember what Mother Teresa said about smile, as quoted below:-

"Smile at others, smile at your spouse, smile at every one, it does not matter who it is – and that will help you grow up in greater love for each other."

It is observed that smile and the world will also smile back at you. Smile reflects your inside. It acts as mirror of your joy and happiness. When accompanied by a smile, your every day expressions – 'How are you?' 'I am glad to see you', etc. are enhanced in value and effect.

Smile is the best prescription for those who find it difficult to laugh. Smile can be simple, spontaneous, joyful, sweet, innocent warm, kind but also cold, cruel and deceptive and mischievous. You have to pick and choose the right kind of smile for the right occasion. There are many professions where smile is an additional qualification. These include stewards, salespersons, receptionists, air-hostess etc. It is good for teacher and politicians too. The smile of a tiny tot and a beautiful women is so charming and captivating.

A smile is a wonderful means to enhance your face value. It does not hurt and can pay you rich dividend. It can make you and others happy and cheerful.

Smile costs nothing but buys many compliments. So keep smiling always.

23. *Be a Learner*

Life is a learning process. Learning comes through reading, through mistakes and experiences of everyday life. One can also learn from teachers, elders and other learned persons. Nature is also a great source of learning. There is no end to education. The whole life, from birth to death, offers a great opportunity to learn.

Always keep learning. Be a good listener, a good observer. Learning involves listening, observing, thinking, reading. It involves full attention, concentration and analysis etc. Let us see, what lord Buddha said about learning as follows:-

'If we did not learn a lot today, at least, we learnt a little, and if we did not learn a little, at least we did not get sick, at least we did not die.'

The process of learning starts right from birth. The baby cries when he is hungry or is in discomfort and gets help. Then he learns to exercise by moving his limbs. As he grows up he learns to sit, crawl, stand, walk and run. As he advances in age he learns many more things either by himself or through the help of others.

In actual life, we should try to learn good things which bring improvement, knowledge, happiness and self-development. We should try to learn all these things, habits and qualities that make us a better individual and a useful citizen.

There is no end to the process of learning. One can learn from books, newspapers, magazines, from friends, from birds and animals and also from natural objects. Travelling is a great source of learning. Every experience in life acts as a source of learning. The process of learning does not end at school, college or university, etc. Therefore, keep learning always.

24. Be an Optimist

There are two sides of a coin. In the same way, any event happening in life may be looked upon in two ways. One gives hope and the other disappointment. One may appear rosy and the other full of thorns. One has optimistic picture and the other pessimistic outlook. There is very big difference between the two views. While optimistic view is positive and beneficial, the pessimistic approach is negative and harmful. One should, therefore be an optimist always.

One should always look forward for the better, even in a bad situation. This is the hallmark of an optimist. A person with an optimistic approach to life can hope for the best even in the worst situation. Optimism brings hope, provides courage and moral strength and makes even a difficult task easier. It becomes the source of success even in the face of failure. An optimist makes efforts with renewed energy and determination. Consequently, he comes out successful in spite of heavy odds.

An optimistic mental attitude gives one several possibilities to excel in life. Failure is not an end of the road and with an optimistic approach, one can make a failure a stepping stone to success. An optimist plans in advance and finds ways and means to achieve success in any endeavour.

The following question from an American writer exhorts as to be an optimist in life:-

"SAY you are well
And all is well with you
God shall hear your words
And make them true."

So be an optimist, trust in God and do your best.

25. Success and Failure

'Success is going from failure to failure without loss of enthusiasm.' **— Winston Churchil**

Winston Churchil who was the Prime Minister of U.K. was one of the most successful persons of his time. The above statement indicates that success and failure go together. According to Swami Chinmaya Nanda, a successful man is one who can lay a firm foundation with the bricks that others throw at him.

Sincem life consists of both success and failure, it is essential to know how to deal with them. In general, one should take all happenings of life in an unagitated and unruffled manner. One need not be flustered with success and unduly dejected in failure. Both the events should be faced with mental poise and equanimity of mind.

While it may be easy and enjoyable to deal with success, it is difficult to face failure. In case of difficulties, one must invoke courage and inner strength to face the challenge. Besides, strong will, determination, and mind control, remembrance of God and practice of meditation are helpful to face failures.

One should learn some thing from each failure. Past mistakes should not be repeated and one need not lament over past failure, but move forward with renewed energy and attain success. In order to be successful one must have the strength of a horse, the skin of an elephant, the eye of a hawk, the alertness of a serpent and the harmlessness of a dove.

Put your mind, heart, intellect, and soul even to your smallest act. This is the secret success. Try to be cheerful and hopeful even in failures.

26. *Follow the Right Path*

LIFE shall become meaningful and purposeful if we follow the right path. But what is the right path?

Man is on the top of all creation. He is endowed with an excellent body, mind and soul complex. His intelligence and wisdom are par-excellence. There is a lot of similarity between the animal and human life. Both eat, sleep, move around procreate. But man's and higher intelligence can distinguish between right and wrong, by virture of which he is expected to do the right. Besides our scriptures also lay down what is right and wrong. All actions based on moral values are right and these determine the right path. These values, inter-alia, include truth, love, non-violence, justice, fellow up kindness, fellowship and compassion etc .

We should, therefore, follow this path which is based on these moral values. This path consists of goodness and godliness. We should have full faith in God and perform all good actions. As a general rule, "we should do unto others as we wish to be done by." In this way we shall lead a happy and contented life and shall also make others happy too. Living the right way means that there is proper coordination and cooperation between our individual and social life. By knowing and following the right path we shall lay the foundation of a better individual and a better world.

27. Love All

Someone has said, "LOVE is the master key that opens the gates of happiness". Another thinker has said, "There is only one happiness in life to love and be loved." Such is the importance of love in life. Without love, life will become barren like a desert sand. If there is one thing that makes life worthy, it is love .

Love has double benefits. By being loving and kind hearted you not only help yourself but also help others come out of difficulties. That is why the sufi poet RUMI said 'If I love myself, I love you. If I love you, I love myself.' Love acts like a soothing balm.

Love is the basis of true religion. It is the expansion of the inner spirit to encompass all virtues. A loving person is kind, considerate, full of compassion, loyal to his commitment and concerned for others. If you are loving all other beings you are truly religious. Love speaks gently. It is far better to rule by love than by fear. Love is the only weapon capable of transforming an enemy into a friend. In short love is the essence of life.

Love leads you towards right thinking and right living. True love is eternal, infinite and unconditional which stands at a higher level.

Love and compassion form the foundation of spiritual life that brings peace and harmony. It can take you beyond your immediate self to a universal level and thus make the world a better place to live.

There is an lrish proverb that says 'We can only learn to love by loving. So love all'. Let us start with our self, our family, our neighbour, our companions, our country and then the whole world and thus live with peace, progress and prosperity.

28. Self Help

"One achieves one's objectives through self-efforts."

— Rigveda

The saying "God helps those who help themselves," applies to all mankind. In human life various objectives are achieved right from day one. After birth a hungry child cries, that acts as a medium of self-help. On hearing his cries, others come to his help. Then he turns and twists, sets, stands, crawls and walks by making self-efforts. Of course he reserves help from others too.

Then the child goes to school and thereafter college and studies, clears his exams and completes his education. In this process major efforts are made by him. After completing education, he finds a job and earns his living and establishes his household after getting married. All these objectives and similar others cannot be attained without making self-efforts.

While making self efforts one gets help from external sources also but the major contribution is one's own. It is also not advisable to depend upon others' help that may or may not be forthcoming at the right time. Dependence upon others may even lead to disappointment and failure. However, one can seek advice from others who are reliable and experienced but the real efforts have to be made by the individual himself.

Self–help creates confidence which is the key to success. The conclusion, therefore, is that self–help is the best help. Therefore make your best efforts and do not depend upon others, as far as possible.

29. Actions and Consequences

Life is full of action and inaction is death. No one remains without performing action.

According to Newton's Law, every action has a reaction. In other words every action produces a result or consequence. The consequence may be good or bad.

The question arises, what sort of action should we perform? The choice is between right and wrong, good or bad. The obvious answer is that we should perform good action are right action. Such actions are expected to be useful for individuals as well as the society. These actions are good, righteous and noble.

The consequences of our actions are not always within our control. Some actions produce immediate results while others may produce results much later or even in another life or next life.

While performing actions, we should concentrate upon our efforts and need not be concerned about what happens. All actions would be performed with detachment and full faith in God who is the dispenser of fruits of all actions. We should accept the consequences of our actions with a calm mind, without any complaint if the result is not favourable. Good results need not make us unduly happy and bad results should not dishearten us. In case of unfavourable results, we should try again with renewed energy.

For all actions, we should keep in mind the philosophy of Karma (Action) as continued in the following verse of the Gita:- "To action you have a right and never at all to its fruits, but not the fruits of action be they motive, neither let there be in thou any attachment to in action."

So perform all actions in the spirit of the above teaching of the Gita.

30. Do not fear Death

Death is inevitable, it is a fact of life. Death is a certainty and no amount of planning can alter its course. The specter of death looms large on almost all individuals. Only a few individuals who are aware of the reality of death are not afraid of it. In general most of us are afraid of death at different stages of life, if not always, in a lesser or greater degree. Human beings also feel sad and aggrieved on the passing away of kith and kin, friends, well-wishers and sometimes even for strangers. Death and the fear of death, both are painful.

Let us consider how the fear of death can be avoided. It is necessary to know the reality of death. The following verse from the Gita shows the way:-

"To the one that is born, death is certain and certain is birth for the one that has died. Therefore for what is unavoidable, thou should not grieve."

Evidently, one should not fear or grieve over what is unavoidable. As death is a normal and natural phenomenon hence there should be no cause for its fear. According to the Gita, death is merely a doorway to another life, so why fear it! In view of this, death at the end of old age should be an occasion to be enjoyed. Death means, one is completing the Journey of life. In real life, completing any kind of journey is a source of satisfaction as one has reached destination. One should understand the fact that in the event of natural and normal death, one has nothing to lose but has to gain as one gets a new fresh body in place of one which is old and decayed.

Having become aware of the reality of death, one need not fear death and be able to say – Life was good, and after death, the new life shall be better. After leading a full life till old age, death delivers us from the pain and misery of old age.

31. *Live your Life Well*

We are born to live life, long or short. Every creature wants to live well. But most of us do not know how to do so and hence are miserable. Human life has two main aspects, material and spiritual. How do we live life, depends upon our actions.

In the material way of life, man wants happiness, success and progress at the physical, social, economic and emotional level through material means which come from wealth and material possessions. He wants to enjoy good health and comforts of material life. In order to do so, he wants to earn more and more money, have more and more of fun and enjoyment, even without caring how he gets there through right or wrong actions.

In spiritual way of life, one has to base his actions on moral rules. He has to follow spiritual practices, yogic discipline, righteousness and has to discriminate between right and wrong.

The material way is very tempting and brings both pleasure and pain while the spiritual way is much more difficult but it can lead to eternal happiness through liberation. Which is the better way of life? Obviously the spiritual way but it is extremely difficult to follow. Only a rare person follows the path. For an average person, the least way is to find a suitable balance between the two. One should enjoy the benefits of material life but within proper limits. He must control his mind and senses and limit his desire. In this way he can practice spiritual discipline side by side and live life well in a desirable manner. Remember that Benjamin Franklin said about life, 'Long life may not be good enough, but a good life is long enough'. Mere living is nothing, but right living is something. So live your life in the right way.

32. *Look for Peace*

PEACE comes to the mind, when there is no disturbance. When the mind is free from worry, fear and anger, peace descends. Peace and freedom cannot be separated. No one can be at peace, unless he has freedom.

Mind is ever fluctuating. It is always restless and runs from one object to another, giving rise to desires. Man who is always engrossed in mundane affairs, in the fulfillment of countless desires is always in search of peace.

There is no peace in the feverish activities of daily life. He runs after achieving various objectives but never feels satisfied with what he achieves. He craves for more. He wants more money, more material possessions, more power and honour more space and so on. In the hectic schedule of life, he does not listen to the inner voice of higher consciousness but listens to his own ego and the worldly clamour around him. He is there for groping in restlessness and never gets peace.

One can get peace by listening to the voice of God who is the source of peace and bliss. One can come closer to God through prayer, meditation, intense love and devotion and total surrender to HIM. One has to discard evil thoughts, actions and intentions. The mind has to be purged of all evil tendencies and designs. Peace brings harmony, inner poise and ultimate bliss.

We should therefore look for peace and imbibe those qualities which being peace. Practice of silent prayer on regular basis, with purity of mind acts as harbinger of inner peace. So look for peace within to ensure self-development.

33. Do your Duty Well

"Every duty is holy and devotion to duty is the highest form of worship." **— Swami Vivekananda**

Every individual has to perform some duty according to his family status, profession and position in the society and the circumstances in which he is placed.

As a child, son or daughter he has to follow instructions of his parents. When he goes to school or collage, his duty is to study hard and respect his teachers. When he enters a profession, it is his duty to work hard and honestly. Then he has duties towards society, country and the world, at large. Thus one has to perform various duties thoughtout life.

Apart from his worldly duties, man has his duty toward God, the creator. A father wants his children to live happily. As God's children we have to establish fellowship and friendly relation with other beings. In order to perform our duty towards God, we should help others who need help, to the best of our capability. Our duty does not be only with ourselves or within our family, but it goes beyond the family ties. We are also required to look and act for the welfare of others also. While doing so, we need not expect anything in return.

In short, we should perform our duty well, full of hope and enthusiasm and to the best of our capacity and capability. In this manner, we shall not only achieve our objective in life, but shall also help our fellowmen, the society and the country besides God. Someone has said "Duty is the sweet daughter of the voice of the soul." So if we do our duty well, we are following the voice of our soul and the voice of GOD.

34. Social Conduct

MAN is a social animal. He can not live in isolation, he has to live with others in the society. The best to do so is to live in harmony and cooperation with others. Our social dealings, should be based on the following dictum:-

"Do unto others as you wish to be done by."

If we follow this advice we shall not harm or hurt others and shall live with them is close cooperation and friendship. If we do not want others to misbehave with us. We should also not misbehave with them. We should treat others in the society with love and respect. Such a behaviour will also engender in them similar feelings of love and goodwill. But all people in the society are not alike. There are many black sleeps and evil doer's also. They have to be dealt with on a different footing. While law of the land should take care of them, we should, as a general rule keep proper distance from them.

As we are children of one and same God, we should try to have loving and friendly relations with others, as far as possible. Of course some exceptions have to be made. We can also judge others from their conduct and then formulate our attitude and dealings with them accordingly.

In general we should be kind and loving in our social conduct. We should refrain from criticising others and need not flare up when others criticise us. We should try to help needy persons and make our contribution of any good cause of social welfare. In this way we shall not only serve the society but shall also help ourselves.

35. *How to Live Life*

We our born to live a full life. Our scriptures tell us to live a life of hundred years. According to current estimate, the average span of life is less then seventy years. This is because we do not know how its live life in the right way.

The following verse from the RIGVEDA provides the guidelines to live life well and fully:-

"Live full life and banish the fear of death from your mind. Resolve to be pure and discard evil thoughts and practices. Be pure in body and spirit and live active life with courage and without fear, follow the path of detachment. God will reward you with happy and prosperous family life."

[Rigveda. 10.18.2.]

The above verse provides guidelines to 'Live life' in a very clear and concise manner. It is essential to acquire quality of purity of body, mind and spirit. We can do so by adopting good and by discarding evil thoughts and actions. Purity is the most important virtue. Both body and mind should be cleansed from outside and inside. Life should be full of action. There is no room for lethargy and laziness. All actions should be righteous and these should be performed with courage and without fear. One should be free from evil thoughts, ignoble desires, temptation, sensual attachments and pleasures of material life.

If we live life in accordance with the above guidelines we shall live life to its fullness and God will grant us peace, prosperity and happiness. What more should we require. Therefore live your life based or these guidelines.

36. Positive Thinking

MAN is a thinking individual. A philosopher has said "You exist because you think you exist". Good thoughts are foundation of life. Character, actions, happiness and everything. If the foundation is strong, life will be healthy, happy and worth living. We should therefore, cultivate good and noble thoughts. Such thoughts are positive and pure thoughts. The importance of such thoughts has been indicated in the following Vedic verse:-

"Let noble thoughts come to us from all sides."—**RIGVEDA**

Broadly speaking, one can think in two ways – positive and negative. Take the example of a glass half full of water. You can either say, It is half full and half empty. The farmer is the case of positive thinking while the later of the negative thought.

Life is full of pleasure and pain. In case of pleasure, we feel happy, smile, laugh and enjoy. In case of pain we feel upset, weep, cry and curse our fate. The latter is the case of negativity. Yes, pain has to be there in life and instead of simply crying we should stand up and face it. We should think of its causes and take courage to remove them. We should take the view that it is a temporary phase and it will pass away and it does pass away as life never stands still. We should do proper thinking and adopt the positive approach as that is the right and beneficial way to deal with bad situations.

Always look at the brighter side of life situation. If you do so, you will face any adverse situation with courage and come out successful at the end. Remember the famous lines of the English poet Shelley who said "If winter comes, can spring be far behind." Thus positive thinking gives us courage and hope to face the adverse situations of life.

37. Find the Way to Bliss

What do we really want from our life?

It may be good health, plenty of wealth, high honour and status in the society, good company, good family, besides all sorts of material pleasures and enjoyments.

Why do we want all these things?

So that we feel happy and comfortable. Now let us see what happens in real life. Some persons may have none of these things, some may have some of these things, only a few may have most of these things. But are people who have most of these things really happy? Again some persons may be happy for sometime, some for more time but none is happy all the time. All have to get pain and punishment more or less. Disease, injury, accident, loss of wealth and honour – all these can happen to anyone anytime. That is why the great GURU NANAK said 'Nanak, Dukhiya, Sab Sansar' (The whole world is miserable). Pleasure and pain are twin sisters. No one can escape from the dualities of life.

So, What is the way out? When we face this question, the search for Divine bliss begins. How do we get that? It is then when we think of GOD, the supreme, the source of bliss as he is SAT-CHIT ANAND. We can get divine bliss through God realization. First of all, we have to achieve full faith in HIM, right faith and not the blind faith. It includes right understanding of GOD, love and full devotion for HIM. Meditation is the path that leads to divine peace. It is an extremely difficult way. While the worldly happiness is transient, the divine, bliss lasting. One can traverse this path with patience, perseverance, blessed by godly inspiration. Let us aspire for it, work hard for it and ultimately attain it.

38. Follow Dharma

All ancient scriptures instruct us to follow dharma. In order to do so, one is required first to understand what is dharma.

Dharma is often equated with traditional religions followed by different people in different forms, like Hinduism. Islamic, Christianity, etc. It may be clarified that the word 'Dharma' has a meaning vaster than the word 'religion', that in common practice is confined to certain beliefs, rituals, forms of worship and so on. Consequently, there are differences among various religions of the world because of our religious beliefs and practices. That is why there are different religions in the world.

DHARMA is a universal concept that is one for all mankind. There is one true religion, but it becomes many as it passes through the human medium. It is the path to God. It is the way of life that brings true happiness in the material world and beyond. It is the relationship between man and God. In the words of M.K. Gandhi, the essence of true religion is morality. In one sentence, dharma may he equated with righteousness, it need not have any sentence or communal name belonging to some specific community or country.

In following dharma, one has to follow the right conduct in thought, word and deed. According to Vedic philosophy a person has to achieve four objectives in life. These are Dharma, Artha (material wealth), Kama (desires) and Moksha (liberation). Dharma is the first and the foremost of the objectives.

Someone has rightly said 'Dharma is living in God, with God and for God'. In real life one can attain material prosperity as well as spiritual happiness by following dharma. Therefore follow dharma in its true sense, always.

39. Avoid Evil Emotions

Human character is a combination of both good and evil traits. While good traits must be cultivated, all evil intentions and emotions should be avoided and kept away.

Lust, anger, attachment, greed, falsehood are the most common evils in human beings. Besides these, are evil emotions like hatred, jealousy etc. that bedevil human mind and behaviour. All these are evils that result from evil emotions and tendencies. Such emotions lead to negative thinking and undesirable action. Consequently, evil emotions bring harm not only to others but also to those who harbour these. Mutual adverse relations, factional fights, communal riots are some of the glaring consequences result from the flush up of evil emotions.

One could control and counter evil emotions by positive ones. For example, hatred can be countered by love, jealousy by praise and sweet talk etc. One has to adopt an attitude of kinship and companionship in order to avoid such evil emotions. We should have concern and compassion for others, as much as we expect for ourselves. All human beings are interconnected by a bond of universal brotherhood and fellowship. Therefore, there should be no cause for evil emotions to arise. We can avoid evil emotions by proper social and cultural interaction.

40. *Have Faith in God*

Some people believe in God, some don't. God is a matter of belief. Those who believe in HIM must have faith in HIM. Those who don't believe in HIM should ponder over following quotations and change their view:-

'If God does not exist, He has to be created.' **— Voltaire**

'God is ever eternal, True lord, Universal spirit. He is and shall be and shall ever remain.' **—Adi Granth**

'God is Life, Truth, Light. He is Love. He is the supreme To me, God is Truth and Love. **—M.K. Gandhi**

'Everyone has the same God; only people differ.'

—Anton Chekhov

'I believe in absolute oneness of God and therefore of humanity.'

—Anonymous

There are numerous other views expressed by other great personalities about the existence of God and his attributes. In short, God is the supreme reality which exists everywhere and for ever. He is the Creator of all that exists,. He is SAT (existence), CHIT (consciousness), ANAND (bliss). He is invisible, but we should try to know HIM through his attributes and on the bears of our holy scriptures which sing his praise.

After knowing the concept of God, we must have full faith in HIM, in thought, word and deed. We should always remember HIM with full faith and devotion. We cannot see God through our eyes but can experience HIM through the practice of meditation and true worship over a long period. We have to surrender ourselves fully before him with love and devotion.

Faith in God does not mean blind faith. We have to actually translate this faith into our actions in life. In other words we have to perform good deeds based on moral values. We have to practice truth, love and non-violence in daily life. Love for all creation is absolute essential.

In real life, true faith in God acts as a great support in our worldly efforts and activities. It can reward us with program, development and happiness in life. If provides inspiration to live our life well and in peace and prosperity.

In short, have full faith in God. Do your best and leave the rest to God, who will take care of all things.

41. Path to Happiness

Everyone in the world wants to be happy. But happiness is a rare commodity and it is difficult to find one who is really happy. Broadly speaking, happiness is of two types. One that is attained through material means and the other through spiritual discipline and practices (Sadhna).

Material happiness is of transient nature, it comes and goes away and gets repeated and lost. It is illusory. One may be happy after eating good tasty food but after sometime may again feel pangs of hunger and become unhappy. Again one may feel happy on acquiring wealth that may get lost after sometime, making him unhappy. A healthy and happy person can become unhappy when he suffers from a disease. In similar way, other good things can make you happy for a while and their loss leads to unhappiness.

The real happiness is the spiritual happiness which is of divine nature. This happiness can be acquired through Gods grace, complete faith, full devotion, self surrender to the supreme are the means to acquire it. One has to practice righteousness and spiritual discipline for a long time. Practicing of rituals, chanting of verses without proper understanding, having blind faith etc are of no avail. It is a difficult path but a rare person can attain it with long practice and the spirit of detachment.

Let us now try to understand and benefit from some of the famous views as quoted below:-

'Self mastery is the greatest conquest, it is the bases of all enduring happiness' — **The Mother**

42. *Practice Charity*

It is said *'Charity is the key to heaven.'* It is the most important tool for spiritual evolution and self-development. Therefore cultivate the noble quality of charity.

In simple language, charity is giving of something useful to a needy deserving person. It is said 'charity is twice blessed.' Both the giver and the recipient get the benefit. The former feels inner satisfaction and happiness while the needs of the latter are fulfilled.

We should always donate for a good cause. Charity can be practiced in different forms. One can donate money, clothes, food, and other household items to the needy poor. In the same way medicines to the sick, books to poor students, scholarship etc can be given as charity.

Charity does not decrease wealth. One may practice charity for different motives, which include, name or fame, praise and admiration or to get some advantage etc. The best charity is that which is given to a deserving person to help him at the proper time and without expectation of anything in return. Indiscriminate alms giving is not true charity. A person who is making exhibition of charity is not doing real charity. Charity should be personal, direct and appropriate.

Charity is a noble act. So try to be charitable and help the poor, the disabled, the orphans and other have-nots. Remember, the hand that gives, gets. Let us become, God's instrument to help others by practicing charity.

43. Avoid Evils

In order to live life well, one should avoid all evils in thought, word and deed. Let us see what Lord Buddha said about evils as quoted below:–

'We must get rid of Ten evils- four of tongue - lying, abusing, slandering and gossiping, three of the mind - desire, envy and hate, and three of the body, - adultry, stealing and killing.

— Lord Buddha

If we shun these evils, our life will be pious, pure and peaceful. Buddha again said 'Let a man avoid evil, as a man who loves life, avoids poison.

In the Gita, lust, greed and anger have been mentioned as three great evils that lead to hell. These evils give rise to many other evils that destroy men and disrupt the society. Corruption, violence and injustice which are rampant in the present day society are the results of these evils.

Evils must be avoided at the initial stage at the individual level. In order to avoid evils, education, knowledge and training are necessary right from the initial stage. Parents and teachers can play an important role in this process. It is said - Idleness acts as a great source of evil. That is why the saying, "An idle man is devil's workshop" One should, therefore, always be engaged in some useful activity. It may be kept in mind that the evil tempts all other men but the idle man tempts the evil. So never remain idle.

Remember the picture of three monkeys of Gandhiji. Below there, was written, "See no evil, speak no evil and do no evil." In conclusion, we can avoid evils if we follow these instructions.

44. Follow the Laws of Nature

All creation is the result of interaction between God and Nature. In order to live life well, we should follow the laws of God and Nature.

Nature is eternally changing, she does not stand still for a moment. Of rest she knows nothing. Nature is in constant flex. Thus change is the fundamental law of nature. Everything is select to change, nothing remains the same as before except God who is always the same and is not subject to change. But He is the cause of all changes.

In view of the evergoing law of change, human beings are required to make necessary adjustments according to the demands of changing realties of life.

The process of change and movement is perpetual. The pendulum of time, the cycle of seasons, the movement of planets, life, wind, water etc. are a few examples of ever-changing nature. Our whole life is a process of change, from birth to death. Changes are always happening in everyday life as one grows from a mere infant to an old man. One has also to encounter seasonal changes. The physical is undergoing change every moment.

In order to live life well, one has to adjust oneself according to the changing situation. One should face pleasure, pain, heat and cold, wealth and poverty, health and disease and confront all these changes with a calm mind and making suitable adjustments and follow the laws of nature.

Everything in excess is opposed to nature. **—Hippocrates**

Nature never deceives us, it is always we who deceive Nature. **—Rousseau**

45. Do Not Be Lazy

According to a verse from the RIGVEDA, God helps only those who work hard with vigour and energy and courage. God does not support those who are lazy and lethargic. The common saying: 'God helps those who help themselves', echoes the same view.

Without making our own efforts, the prayer and the worship of god is of no avail. A person who is lazy and makes no efforts does not deserve God's help. As the saying goes 'Work is worship.' Every piece of work, performed with best possible efforts becomes worship. The following quotation about laziness can act as our good guide:–

"From rust, from disuse
Stagnant water, loses its purity.
In cold weather, water gets frozen.
Like wise, laziness, saps the rigour of the body and the mind"

The above verse shows the ill effects of laziness. A lazy person loses health, wealth and happiness. He can become a victim of several diseases, hunger and poverty. He is also mocked by others and loses their love and respect.

Therefore remain active, keep busy and energetic and never be lazy.

46. Help the Needy

Man is a social animal. While living in the society, it is his primary duty to help his fellowmen who are needy. In the society, there are rich and poor, high and low, healthy and sick people. When we are in need of something we look to others for help and get their help. In the same way, we should also help the needy people. The rich should help the poor, the healthy should comfort the sick, and those who are literate should help the illiterate and so on.

One can help others in many ways. We can offer financial help, clothes, food etc. to the needy poor who lack these things. We can also provide medicine to the sick people and look after their other needs. There are also other ways of giving help to others. The following quote from BENJAMIN FRANKLIN will provide some guidelines:-

"The best way to give your enemy is forgiveness; to your opponent, tolerance, to a friend, your ear, to your child, good example, to your father, reverence and to your mother, conduct that will make her proud of you; to yourself respect, to all men charity."

Giving help to others is not a bad bargain. Infact giving is getting, If you give love, you with get it in return, if you respect others, they will also help you. Just and unselfish giving will bring you satisfaction and joy. Besides, God will surely bestow his kindness upon you in due course. Thus by giving help to the needy, you are not only helping them, but helping yourself too.

47. *Distinguish Between Virtue and Vice*

Virtue and vice are perfectly bound together in human life. Falsehood, wickedness, jealousy, greed and anger etc generally live together with truth, wisdom, nobility and contentment, etc. Similarly, joy and sorrow, pleasure and pain are woven together in the fabric of human life.

Most virtues of human nature may be condensed into thoughtfulness, right actions and goodwill for all. Major writers include endurance, patience, self-control, integrity, purity, restraint of the senses, wisdom, learning, truth and non-anger. Vices are the opposite of virtues and include anti-social habits like stealing, violence, drug addiction etc. Virtue is its own reward, here in this life, as you grow by it. Vice is its own punishment, here on earth, as it hinders growth. According to ADI GRANTH, "All vices are like chains around the neck."

Man is at the top of all creation. He is far above the animal level as he is endowed with the power of making distinction between right and wrong. While virtues should be adopted and practiced as it is right to do so and vices should be avoided and discarded as these are wrong, distructive and negative. We should therefore, make a proper distinction between right and wrong, virtue and vice. In short, practice virtues and shun vices.

48. *Do Not Grumble*

WHY do people often grumble?

They do so when something happens that is not to their liking, something unfavourable, etc. One often grumbles over the shortage or the absence of resources and material possessions, over sickness etc. Oh, I don't have a car, a house, good clothes, nice food and so on. It is the desire to have more and more of money which is behind most of the causes for grumbling. When one fails to get wealth or good health and is unable to fulfill one's desires and needs, one often grumbles.

One also grumbles when something undesirable happens. For example, one may fall sick, meet an accident, fail an examination or fail to get promotion or lose something etc. Sometimes, we grumble out of jealousy when we compare our adverse situations with others' good luck. Sometimes we grumble over hot or cold weather etc. Thus there may be many more reasons for grumbling.

In order to avoid grumbling, one must think over and understand that grumbling is a negative property and it should be avoided. It is of no use and it does not help, at all. One must analyse the situation and try to remove the cause that leads to grumbling. In all adverse situations, you should exercise restraint, patience and contentment. There should be no cause for grumbling, if one feels satisfied with what one gets after making ones best efforts. If one is not satisfied, he should put in more hard work and he will be duly rewarded sooner or later.

So never grumble, if you do so,
You will stumble!
Put in your best, And leave the rest to God –
He will Never let you crumble.

49. *Cross over Hardships*

The Journey of life does not run its course in a straight line. It is beset with several curves and round abouts, twist and turns, hurdles and hardships. There are diseases, deficiencies, disaster and several other difficulties in different forms and shapes. Thus life is a continuous struggle full of adversities and adventures mixed with pleasant and painful experiences. It is a constant battle against evils, disturbances and distractions. There is no escape from obstacles, hurdles and hardships.

One has to face all these challenges and adverse situations boldly with courage. One has to fight on two fronts, against external adverse forces and the evils within. All the hardships must be faced and crossed over, with determination and righteous resolves. While facing hardships with full self-confidence, one must always keep God in mind and seek his inspiration and guidance. In this way, a safe passage through all impediments of life can be assessed.

'Trust in God and do the right' should be the motto to face all hardships of life. One should also seek friendly human help wherever available. This is the way to cross over all hurdles and hardships and come out successful.

50. Acquire Knowledge

Knowledge is not mere information; it is a matter of actual experience. If you have read about milk but have never seen or drunk it, you will not really know about it unless you drink it. The first step to acquire knowledge is to know that we are ignorant. This creates the need to know and then you will try to know actually. To eat, one has to first feel hunger and then he will look for food, try to get and eat it. We need to acquire knowledge because we do not know something and thus there is need to know that. The thirst for knowledge has to be there.

To attain knowledge, one has to make efforts and acquire more and more information about things, places, men and matters, arts and sciences and so on. Knowledge is mainly of two types, material and spiritual. Material knowledge leads to material progress, development and material comforts and happiness while spiritual knowledge brings libration and eternal bliss. Material knowledge can be gained through the process of learning and education while spiritual knowledge comes through God's grace. While material knowledge is deserved from external sources, spiritual knowledge comes from within, through introspection, prayer, meditation etc.

All knowledge is inferior to self knowledge. 'He who knows others is clever; he who knows himself is enlightened' [Tao Tzu] says the Chinese philosopher. Knowledge is the powerful armour to safeguard you always. A proverb says "A little knowledge is a dangerous thing." He who knows the least, presumes the most. If you thoroughly know anything, you should teach it to others.

It is said 'Knowledge is ecstatic in enjoyment, perennial in fame, unlimited in space and infinite in duration'.

51. *Lead a Happy Life*

Life is not a period of mourning; it is an opportunity to celebrate and enjoy happiness. Our scriptures instruct us to live life with happiness for a hundred years and meet its end like a ripened fruit falling from a tree without any fuss.

Human life is most precious and a special gift of God to mankind. He who does not get fun and enjoyment out of it needs to reorganize his life. One must plan and live life in such a manner that one gains good beneficial experiences and thus leads a virtuous and happy life. Life can be tough but if you know the art to laugh at it, you have the ability to enjoy it. Each day is little life, so plan each day to live happily.

Life is a short enough affair; it is too short for us to make it petty, cheap and unhappy. Life begins afresh every morning, so make full use of it to live well. It should not be wasted in evil pursuits which would cut the life span. One should perform ones duties honesty, bravely and go through its various stages peacefully and progressively. One must lead a disciplined life based on moral values and righteous practices.

Pt. J.L. Nehru said 'Life is like a game of cards. You have no control over the hand that is dealt to you, the way you play your cards depends upon you'. Someone has said 'A long life may not be good enough, but a good life is long enough.' So try to play your cards well and make it a happy, enjoyable and fulfilling experience. It does not matter whether it is short or long as the duration of life is not in our hands, but how we live it mainly depends upon us.

52. *Fair Means*

"As the means, so the end.
Ahimsa is the means, truth is the end." **—M.K. Gandhi**

"So long as we do not adhere to right means, the end will not be right and fresh evil will flow from it." **—J.N. Nehru**

The importance of fair means is indicated in these thoughts of two greatest Indians of modern age. So long as the means are right, the end will be good.

Everyone wants to acquire wealth to lead a good happy life. But wealth should not be obtained through foul and unfair means. Such wealth does not enhance real happiness and also does not last long.

Why should one adopt unfair means to acquire more and more wealth? It is the attitude of Greed that impels people to do so. Greed is the mother of many evils. It can lead to violence, theft, robbery, murders and similar other crimes and unsocial acts. It leads to excesses and one must remember that excess of everything is bad. One should, therefore try to live and manage within his honest resources and need not adopt unfair means to hoard more and more wealth, material possessions, power, honour or status etc.

Desires make man greedy and excess of wealth results in false pride, indulgence in sensual pleasures, besides it can also lead to violent and unjust action. Excessive enjoyment of worldly pleasures enhances greed which destroy inner peace and happiness.

In order to ensure good results, the means must be right. One should, therefore, adopt fair means to achieve good results.

53. Be Polite

There is a saying "Courtesy costs nothing but buys everything."

This shows the importance of being polite. During conversations, one should make use of sweet and pleasant words for mutual benefits and to avoid bad feeling and unpleasant situation.

Never speak harsh words and let not bitter words and abuse come out of your lips at any time. It is said that physical injury and wounds can heal after sometime but hurts inflicted by bitter words last for a long time. Harsh words create bitter feelings and anxiety even among friends and fellow beings. Impolite words destroy mutual goodwill and it is often difficult to erase them from your memory. We should, therefore, avoid rough and tough language in our everyday dealings and social life. We should also try to keep away from such people who use impolite language.

Being polite, however, does not mean bowing before evil minded people who try to browbeat others by using harsh words and abuses. With them, one need not be impolite, but should be firm, straightforward and should practice plain speaking, without picking up quarrel. One should avoid exchange of impolite speech, on such occasions, as far as possible. We should try to convince them against their impolite conduct through our politeness and patience.

So be polite within the limits of truth and propriety. Do justice and fair play while dealing with your fellow beings. Politeness should be inculcated among children, within home, school and college, so that they shall become good and responsible citizens as they grow up in life.

54. Always Work Hard

Hard work is the key to acquire wealth and success in all walks of life. Good future follows those who are industrious and hardworking. Lazy people who do nothing and waste time in idle pursuits do not achieve anything in life. They are left behind cursing their bad luck while energetic and hard working people excel and reach their goal.

Hard work should be rightly directed towards a beneficial goal. There should be proper planning for the proposed work. One should acquire more and more useful knowledge about the job to be done and then apply best efforts to attain success. When you do hard work, doors keep opening and success is assessed.

God created man to work which is his greatest duty. The great hindrances to work are:– sleep, sluggishness, fear, anger and procrastination. Never put off till tomorrow, what you can do today. Remember, well begun is half done. So start your work with good intentions, right spirit, appropriate zeal and proper planning.

One should not feel disheartened if hard work, sometime does not produce expected results. One has to try again and again and thus achieve good results through more hard work. In case of some failure, we should seek advice and proper guidance from those who had achieved success in life through persistent hard labour.

Hard work always pays rich dividends, sooner or later. It is the right means of self-help and self-development which bring success in life.

55. *Cultivate Friendship*

Man is a social animal and he has to live in the society with others.

As such he has to find some associates whom he can call friends. A friend in need is a friend indeed. True friends are those who come and share your happiness when we call them, and our misfortunes, without being called. A true friend is one of life's great assets. A real friend is one who walks in, when rest of the world walks out. Hold a true friend with both hands. Beware of friends who merely flatter you and who are only fair weather friends.

One should cultivate friendship with true friends who have been tested and are trustworthy and reliable, affectionate and helpful. The only way to have a friend is to be one first. We are like travellers in the world and the best that we can find in our journey is an honest friend. Such a good man can be the best friend and therefore soonest to be chosen, longer to be retained and never to be parted with.

Friendship may be cultivated between like natures, only such friendship can be worthy and enduring. 'True friendship is an identity of soul' – said M.K. Gandhi. Friendship should be cultivated with great ease and caution. The friendship of one whose family background, character and values are not known should not be cultivated as it is very risky and harmful to do so. True friendship is like sound health, its value is not known until it is lost.

Friendship can flourish between caring husband and wife, father and children, among relatives and other fellow beings who are honest, loving and Godfearing. Cultivate friendship with good people as it can lead to mutual benefit and happiness.

56. *Healthy Body and Healthy Mind*

Body, mind and the soul are wonderful assets of a human being. Body and mind are a vehicle for the soul. As body and mind affect each other, these must be kept in a healthy and happy state. It is said that a healthy body has healthy mind.

Man is at the top of creation because no other creature is endowed with such magnificent assets as a human being has. The body must be kept fit and fine so that the mind maintains its peace and progress. One must take care of one's body by avoiding all external and internal adversaries. If is essential to take healthy food, do proper physical exercise, maintain healthy lifestyle and follow the fundamentals of good health.

Regarding mind, the great English poet MILTON said, 'The mind is its own place, and in itself can make a heaven of hell and hell of heaven.' It should always be enriched and energized with positive thoughts and by practicing good habits and moral values. Reading of good literature, good company, self-analysis, meditation etc are good means to keep the mind healthy and in good shape. It is not enough to have a good mind, the main thing is to use it well. Therefore, the mind should always be kept engaged in useful healthy and positive pursuits. It should not remain idle, as an idle mind becomes devil's workshop.

We should also seek divine inspiration and intervention for keeping our body and mind in healthy and happy state. Righteous conduct, prayer and meditation are useful means for this purpose. Always remember God and remain grateful to him. A philosopher has said 'There is no more pleasing exercise of the mind than the expression of gratitude.'

57. *Living Together*

We are all children of God.

God is the creator, our supreme father. The brotherhood of mankind rejoin upon us the duty to live together with other beings peacefully and happily.

Scriptures tell us that the whole world is like one family. God instructs all human beings to live together in an atmosphere of love, friendship and peace. We should release the fact that all living beings have similar soul, so we are not different from one another.

The best way to live together is to follow the dictum– 'Do unto others as you wish to be done by'. In this way, we shall behave with others in the same manner as we should like them to behave with us. As such there would be no cause for conflict and we shall live together with love and mutual affection.

A feeling of camaraderie among all human beings should form the basis of living together. The spirit of mutual companionship will enable us to share our joys and sorrows together. Human life will become a sharing enterprise of love and friendship. In short, while living together like one family, we shall be good and helpful to our fellow beings. There shall be no feelings of jealousy and hatred among mankind and this world shall become a better and worthy place to live in. There is an ideal that we can achieve by living together.

58. *Make your own Decisions*

In our life, we are always faced with different issues and problems at different times, when one has to take a decision one way or the other. It is often to fend oneself at crossroads during various stages of life. Human life is like that and there is no escape from such situations.

At the educational and professional level, one has to take a major decision as it would affect the career. One has to decide which course to decide and which profession to follow. In view of the tremendous competition and plethora of educational courses, this poses a big problem. Similarly getting married and selecting a life companion is another major decision of life. Then there is big question of choosing your friends and associates. There are several other situations in life when taking a decision poses some problem.

Some people always depend upon others for taking different decisions. This is not desirable. One may take advice and necessary guidance from other helpful sources, but should take one's own decision after taking into account appropriate information and pros and cons of any decision to be taken in any given situation. People who depend more on others for taking there decisions develop a slavish mentally and lose self-confidence. They can be misguided also and thus come to harm.

One should, therefore, try to take one's own decision after due thought, proper inputs and analysis of the particular situation and finally arrive at his own considered decision, without any wavering once a decision has been taken, one should put in best efforts to implement it and leave the rest to the grace of GOD.

59. *Simple Living*

'Simple living and high thinking' should be the motto of life.

Simple living implies long life in a natural way, without artificiality and ostentation, practising humanitarian principles of love, truth, non-violence, fellow feelings etc. There should be absence of falsehood, greed, deception, cunningness etc in the simple way of living.

One can live life at these levels, personal, social and spiritual. At the personal level one should cultivate good habits based on moral values. At the social level one should cultivate good conduct based on love, kindness, friendship and concern for others. At the spiritual level, we should love God and practice godliness.

When one adopts simple life-style, one eats simple natural foodstuff, one dresses in a simple manner, mainly to protect the body in an appropriate manner; cultivates good sociable manners and keeps away from discord, unnecessary discussions, back-biting etc. One adopts a helpful and loving approach towards others in the family and in the society.

A practitioner of simple living and high thinking is God fearing but otherwise fearless, has fellow feelings and is loving, kind and compassionate. He does not indulge in wild gossip, angry argumentation and fruitless discussions etc. He is always willing to help others without any expectation of praise or any prize. He does not have false pride but believes in self-respect and respects others.

Simple living and high thinking can make life happy, peaceful and purposeful.

60. Adjust and Cooperate

Man can not live in a vacuum; he has to live with others in the society.

Everyone has his own views, thinking, aims and objects. As such, he wants to do various thinking in his own way and as it suits him. In this way, he may try to thrust his own views upon others and also try to act according to his desire and inclinations. Such an attitude can create conflict and contradiction among members of the same family, among neighbours, among members of the society with whom he comes into contact.

In real life situation, we can not always expect others to agree with our views and actions. In the society it is very difficult that all people should think about a particular subject or situation. There are always individual differences. In such a scenario and in order to avoid conflict, we should adopt the practicable course of mutual adjustment and cooperation. While we have every right to express our candid views on any subject, it is our duty also to listen to what others have to say on the some subject. In this manner, we can find a via-media to solve the problem being faced by us. Mutual discussion and proper reasoning can lead the way to an acceptable approach through consensus.

We should always keep in mind that in the society or in the family, we have to co-exist with others in spite of our individual differences. Proper adjustment and mutual cooperation are the vital means to co-exist peacefully and happily.

61. *Give and Take*

We cannot do everything ourselves always. It therefore becomes necessary to seek the help from wherever possible. While we seek help from others, in the same way, it is our duty also to help others when they need it. This process of 'Give and take' forms an essential aspect of human life.

There should be no hesitation in seeking help from others who are willing to do so. Similarly, we should also be ready to help others who seek our help.

By helping others, we get satisfaction of having done something worthwhile. There are many ways of helping others. It may be in the from of money, food, medicine, clothing etc. Apart from material help a word of consolation and encouragement, giving of knowledge, sharing of useful information etc are also useful ways to help others. It is not necessary, that one has to give something material always. One can help an old person to cross the road or to board a bus or carry some load to his home or fetch some medicine or other household item for an elderly neighbour etc. Even small gestures can make a big difference.

There is a Vedic mantra which says that you could earn by hundred hands and give by a thousand hands. Giving does not reduce your wealth, it will come back in greater proportion by divine law. Do not feel bad if your giving is not praised or recognized. Remember, virtue is its own reward. But you should always feel grateful if you take something from somebody. Your expression of gratitude will create good feelings in the giver.

Therefore make 'Give and Take' a daily practice of your life.

62. *Concentrate on your Job*

Concentration means paying your wholehearted attention one thing at a time. It increases the strength of the body and the mind while performing a given task. It enhances the efficiency and the speed of whatever you do. Honesty, efficiency and concentration are the three main factors for achieving success in any job.

The process of concentration involves application of total attention to whatever you are doing. If you are walking, talking, reading, writing, eating, cleaning, driving etc, be wholly absorbed in that particular act. In this way you will not only enjoy doing it, but also shall do it in a better way.

In the beginning it may be difficult to concentrate. One may practice concentration and gradually increase its duration. It is said that 'practice makes a man perfect.' The same principle applies here. By regular constant practice, one can increase the power of concentration and achieve the desired results.

Scientists, writers, thinkers, holy men and other successful persons in different fields have achieved marvellous results by exercising concentration. Sportspersons, athletes, research scholars have attained wonderful achievements through the power of concentration.

As concentration can make your efforts successful and more fruitful, you should make it your motto while performing any work in your daily life.

63. Practice Auto Suggestion

It is an acknowledged fact that our mind controls our body. With the power of thought, one can make hell of heaven or heaven of hell. The power of thought can be energized and enhanced through the practice of auto suggestion. The power of auto suggestion can fight disease, improve health, achieve success in an enterprise and bring self-development.

The magic mantra of auto suggestion is to keep saying in the mind 'I can do it.' In this way one can enhance one's physical and mental capacity to perform better in any job. The sub-conscious mind has the power to heal and maintain good mental and physical health. However it needs prompting to produce the results. It is here that the role of auto suggestion comes into play.

In case you are in a bad situation, give a powerful thought to your mind that you can come out of it. Simultaneously you have to make successful efforts to improve the situation. In this way even a bad situation can be improved upon. The first steps to auto suggestion is to be in a relaxed frame of mind so that it is in a willing state to receive your positive instructions. A relaxed mind will receive auto suggestion in a better and effective manner.

For self-development, one has to make positive and beneficial auto suggestions. If you want to avoid the dirty habit of smoking you have to instruct your mind constantly– 'Smoking is bad.' I will stop smoking etc. Many people have stopped smoking or drinking by practicing auto suggestion. Similarly, auto suggestion can bring success and produce beneficial results in other ventures.

64. Control your Ego

EGO is the most common weakness of man. It produces selfishness, false pride, hypocrisy, jealousy and hatred etc. A man full of ego would like to influence others by argumentation and will thus feel superior to others. Such a person will think that only he is right and others are wrong. He becomes jealous of other people's wisdom. Egoism can create conflict among members of the society and this can spread hatred and harm.

One should shun this bad habit. In order to do this, one has to analyse and introspect. One need not speak ill of others and avoid unnecessary criticism of others. One should remember God in a spirit of self-surrender and humility. One should also not feel proud of one's wealth and material possessions. Instead one should feel humble and try to help the needy people and encourage them to go better.

Egoist people are very fond of bragging. They will often stress their point of view by saying 'It is my firm view'. 'I did this or that' and so on. They will always try to exhibit their own importance. Self-centeredness is a sign of a narrow mind-a lower level of consciousness. One should avoid such attitude and should think, act and behave like one who is a part and parcel of whole creation and thus live with others in a spirit of equality, fellowship and camaraderie.

Always keep in mind, the following quotation from SATYA SAI BABA and control your ego:-

"Just as a big pot full of water is emptied by a small hole even a little ego will burn up all the nobility of a good heart."

65. *Aspire for Peace and Happiness*

PEACE and HAPPINESS reside together.

One cannot be happy without inner peace. Most people seek peace and happiness through material objects, sensual gratification, fulfillment of desires etc. In this process they try to get more and more, feel restless, become angry and afraid and then lose both peace and happiness. Desires and fear are two enemies of peace and happiness. One should, therefore limit one's desires and have no fear.

Peace and happiness do not arise out of material objects and sensual allurements. Even if one feels happy in material comforts and possessions, such happiness is mixed with fear and also does not last long. Peace and happiness reside in a pure mind and soul. Happiness obtained through external sources is short lived and is followed by pain and misery. Worldly pleasure and pain go together.

Happiness and sorrow are the varying states of the mind that keep fluctuating from one end to another. Peace prevails when the wavering of the mind stops. Peace and happiness reside in the mind. In order to acquire peace and happiness one should have control over the mind. Good conduct, love for God and his creation, prayer and meditation are the means to control the mind. One has to practice this discipline over a long time in a spirit of detachment. When control over the mind is established, peace prevails and where there is peace, there is happiness.

66. *This Shall Pass Away*

Human life is a complex combination of pleasure and pain. Where there is happiness, there is misery too. While everyone welcomes pleasure and happiness, it becomes very difficult to bear pain and face misery. Good time seems to pass away very soon, but time of pain and sorrow looms large for a long time. While happy time is full of fun and enjoyment, how should one spend time of pain and misery.

In times of adversity and distress, there is no escape and one has to endure these hard ships willy nilly. But there is a positive way to deal with such situations. One should repeatedly feed the mind with one forceful thought by saying, "Yes there is difficulty but this shall pass away." By doing so the effort of pain will decrease and one can hopefully look towards better time. It is said "Hope sustains life." There is always dawn after the dark night and the sunshine of hope shall make the pain slide away.

Look at the natural cycle of seasons. The great English poet Shelley said 'If winter comes can spring be far behind.' The difficulty faced in the sweltering summer heat passes away and is followed by mild less warmer season. Again the ferocity of cold winter passes away with the coming of comfortable spring season. In the same way, the pendulum of pleasure and pain, joy and sorrow etc swing in opposite directions and brings relief.

Do not take your moments of pain too gravely and say to yourself. "This shall pass away." If you are optimistic and entertain positive attitude, bad time does pass away to be replaced by better time.

67. *You Should not Run Away*

When things go wrong as they sometimes will,
When the road you are trudging seems all uphill,
When the funds are low and the debts are high,
And you want to smile, but you have to sigh,
When case is pressing you down a bit
REST if you must but don't quit.
Life is queer with its twists and turns
An everyone of us sometime learns,
And many failures turn about,
When he might have won, had he stuck it out,
Don't give up though the space seems slow!
You may succeed with another blow!
Success is failure turned inside out.
The silver tent of the clouds of doubt,
And you never can tell how close you are.
It may be near when it seems so far.
So stick to the fight when you are hardest set,
It is when things seem worst, that you must not quit.

[ANONYMOUS]

68. *Live a Detached Life*

We live in a world full of temptations and attractions and most human beings get stuck in the sticky mud of these allurements of the material world. In this way, they waste their precious life in the turmoil and tribulations of worldly attachments. The better way to live life is to live in the world practicing detachment. The example of LOTUS flower is before us. It is born in mud but rises above it and blooms in clean space above and spreads its fragrance.

One can lead a detached life amidst attractions, by practicing the art of detachment and yet be dynamic and actively engaged in the activities of the world. Detachment does not necessarily mean leaving the household and returning to a forest etc. It means not to get stuck in the mundane allurements. One can remain calm, unperturbed and unattached while going through various worldly activities and enticements.

The best way to practice detachment is to limit your desires and to control the mind from wavering. One has to introspect and look within, rather than outside, to know the reality of life. Human greed is the greatest obstacle against detachment. We should practice contentment and make our life need-based and not greed-based as greed has no limit while our needs can be kept within proper limit and even reduced to a minimum level.

There are several benefits of living a detached life. It is free from feverish activity and unnecessary disturbance. It can bring peace, real joy and happiness. What more do you want?

69. *How to Start your Day?*

There is a saying *'Well begun is half done.'*

If you begin your day well, the whole day will pass off well. Our daily life should have an early start. One should get up early in the morning well before sunrise, say between 5 to 6 AM. During summers, one can get up even earlier. Some people may like to get up even earlier. But awakening late after sunrise is a sign of laziness, unless someone has some special reason for doing so.

Always start your day with some morning prayer which should be in the nature of thanksgiving to the supreme power and seeking his inspiration for a better day. Spend sometime in meditation which will bring peace and stillness to the mind. This can be a good start to begin your day.

After attending to your morning needs, go out for morning walk in a neighbourhood park or in any open space where fresh air and some greenery is around and birds are singing their morning song. A brisk walk for about 30-45 minutes would do good to your health. One can also do some physical exercise to activate one's limbs. One can also meet and have some chit-chat with other people also.

After attending to your morning needs, the day opens up for professional work. You should do your work in the spirit of 'KARMA YOGA'. In simple words, do your work honestly and to the best of your capacity. No time should be wasted. The motto should be "Work is Worship."

On return from work, one should have some refreshments relax a bit one, interact with other family members. One can go for evening walk, if possible, and meet friends, neighbours etc. It is not good to watch T.V. for a long time. One should see only selected programs.

After taking light dinner, followed by a cup of milk etc one should go to bed early, not later than to 10 p.m. Remember the saying “Early to bed and early to rise, makes a man, healthy, wealthy and wise.” At the time of going to bed, one should again say some prayer and do some meditation and enjoy a peaceful night, to rise again for the next morning.

70. *Do not Sit Idle*

"An idle mind is the devil's workshop."

The message of the above proverb is – "Do not remain idle." There is an oriental proverb which says – 'Do not sit without work, do something. If you have nothing else, unstitch your clothes and stitch them again.' The moral of this old proverb is that always keep doing something.

Life is short and very precious. It is not meant to idle away time and waste it. We have to perform some duties assigned to us due to our birth or by way of profession. We should therefore make the best use of this time and perform our duties well and usefully. As time runs very fast, we must make use of every moment purposefully. Death is inevitable and it can come anytime. Therefore, the time at our disposal should not be wasted in idle gossip, idle pursuits or by doing anything at all! Time lost never comes back and one can only repent upon time wasted in idleness.

Some people always keep running around here and there in idle pursuits or in several enjoyments which are only short-lived and require repetition. These do not bring about any positive, constructive results. This involves only waste of precious time which is part of our priceless life. Human life is a precious gift of God to man, it should be properly utilized to attain purposeful and beneficial objectives.

To sum up, do not remain idle. Always be engaged in some constructive and creative useful activity either for self-development or for the service of the society.

71. Make Best use of Nature's Gifts

Human life is the most precious form of life and God has given many precious gifts to man to make the best use of them. Some of the main precious gifts are as follows:-

EARTH – This is the place where human beings are born to live and work. It provides us with food and several other products without which we cannot survive or live properly. It also gives us several lessons, stability, strength, tolerance, patience, productivity and so on.

WATER – We cannot survive long without water. Vegetables, pulses, fruits and other food articles won't grow without water which is also very useful in several other ways. It keeps moving and is flexible and has great strength and energy. It teaches these values to mankind.

AIR – It is one of the most useful and powerful aid for life. It provides the breath of life and can be used in many ways to sustain life and to make it more useful.

FIRE – It provides heat and light and purifies everything. We use it to keep our body warm and healthy and to cook our food. It has numerous other uses in science and industry. A man becomes dead when the heat in the body is lost.

SKY/SPACE – It provides the limitless covering which spreads over the universe. It is the home for the sun, the moon and many other plants. Perhaps the universe wont survive without this cover.

These five elements are most vital for universal existence. These are the most precious natural gifts which come free from God. We must keep them pure and in their natural fresh state and try to make the best use of these gifts.

72. Silence and Solitude

Modern life has become so hectic, engaged in everyday activities that there is little scope for rest and peace of mind. There are scores of household chores to do, personal, professional, social and so on. In this scenario, one may be forced to say– What is this life if full of care, we have no time to stand and stare!

If you meet anyone the road side, you may hear him saying "Oh I have no time, I have to do this and that." The humdrum of life makes man moving, running and restless, most of the time. In general man feels disturbed, restless and disillusioned most of the time. What is the solution to get out of this undesirable mode?

The solution lies in the practice of silence and solitude. Many people are fond of talking endlessly. This can become a cause of tension, stress and even discord among companions. In order to avoid stress, one must practice silence, at least for sometime, everyday. One can sit in complete silence in some corner of the house, on roof top, or some where in a park. This can he done at different time of the day, in the morning, at night etc.

Silence conserves mental energy. It is also beneficial for the physical body and the mind. To practice silence, one must first try to speak less and wherever you have to speak, do it in a low, sweet voice and for a short time. One must avoid, undesirable gossip, loose talk, and unnecessary discussion.

In order to show the importance of silence some thoughts of great thinkers are quoted below:-

The real rest is in the inner life, in peace and silence.
The real rest must be an ascent into perfect peace,
total silence. **—Sri. Aurobindo**

"Experience has taught me that silence is part of the spiritual discipline of a votary of truth." **—M. K. Gandhi**

"Silence restores the body as the nest energies birds at rest." **—R. N. Tagore**

"Silence helps in winning over anger to the extent that on other thing can." **—M. K. Gandhi**

"The highest form of grace is silence.

—Chinmaya Nanda

'Silence is the best answer to the stupid.'

'Silence is the beginning of wisdom.'

'The wisest retort is silence.'

'Out of purity and silence, comes the word of power.'

—Chinmaya Nanda

In view of the great value of silence, we should practice silence for our self development and success in life.

73. Observe Patience and Self-Restraint

Some people blurt out anything or do anything instantly without any forethought and without thinking about the consequences of what they say or do. This is because they have no patience and no control over their mind. Such people can always find themselves in some trouble or tension. They remain agitated and restless and this can lead them to difficult situations. What should they do?

For them the solution lies in exercising patience and self-restraint. Patience is the best remedy for every trouble. It helps in overcoming most adverse situations. Those who practice patience and self-restraint, think twice before uttering a word or taking some action. Patience precedes self-restraint and by observing it a person becomes confident and successful. These enhance will power and strength of the mind. Self-restraint can make you look around before you leap and observance of patience can save you from various adverse situations.

Here are some quotations which show the importance and utility of patience and self-restraint:-

— *Patience is the best remedy for every trouble.*

— *Patience indeed is the ally of progress.*

— *There is no life without HOPE and no future without patience. Patience is a commitment to the future.*

— *Self-conquest is greater than all other conquests.*

— *Moral results can only be produced by moral restraint.*

—M. K. Gandhi

In conclusion patience and self-restraint are very valuable aids in material as well in the spiritual domain. We must therefore practice these qualities in all walks of life.

74. Past, Present and Future

TIME is the stuff that life is made of. It is said 'Time is life and life is time.' Time is always flying but we can divide it into three periods — past, Present and Future. Present is the time we are facing, Past has gone by and future is yet to arrive. If we think deeply, time is always in the present. It was the present time that has rolled into the past and the future will also become present.

In view of the importance of the present time, we should always live in the present time and make use of it judiciously. We should use our time for our good and for the good of others. The great philosopher BENJAMIN FRANKLIN said "If you love life, then do not squander time. We should make the best use of the PRESENT time". We need not keep brooding over the past and worrying over the future. Past is dead and gone no riches can bring it back. But we can learn some useful lessons from the past happening and use them for our present welfare. Past mistakes should not be repeated. If we take care of our present, the future will take care of itself. It is in the present time that we can plan for our future. Future is always unknown and uncertain; therefore we need not unnecessarily worry about it.

Remember the following thoughts about the time:-

Time is money, time is life.
Time flees; it marches on.
Catch time by the fore lock.
Time and tide wait for none.
Today is forever, forever is today.

In view of the great importance of the PRESENT, make the best use of TODAY. Do not put off till tomorrow, what you can do today.

75. *Do not Delay*

Some people have the habit of delaying what they would or are required to do well in time. They always think 'What is the hurry, it can be done later on.' This is due to their laziness or the habit of procrastination which is a bad habit. Procrastination means postponement till tomorrow what can be done today.

Whatever is required to be done today should be done at an early stage: it should not be put off till another day unless there are some genuine reasons to do so. Those who do not postpone or delay their work, achieve success and also win the appreciation of their superiors. There is a saying, 'A stitch in time, saves nine.'

A job done well in time, without delay, brings satisfaction and great relief to the doer as well as to the person for whom it is done. A work delayed becomes a burden on the head; it can cause unnecessary worry and may be done badly or even end in failure. In such a case one will always remain under stress and will say 'Oh, I have not done this or that'! This creates fear, tension and anxiety that can add to the problem.

If we keep on delaying many things, laziness will become our habit. It is, therefore always desirable and useful not to delay any work which has to be done. It is better to do it earlier than later. If we do our work only at the eleventh hour, it will call for more efforts and make an easier task much more difficult. 'Let us do it now' should be the motto for the performance of work in our daily life.

76. Do not be Selfish

'Selfishness is the greatest curse on human race'.

— Gladstone

Most people in our world live shut in their cocoon. They always think of themselves or their family and have no concern for others. Their approach to life is narrow and restricted within the fear walls of their household. They think of only their pleasure, profit and happiness and do not bother to help others for their welfare.

A human being is endowed with superior intelligence and several other qualities of head and heart. He is at the top of God's creation. He is supposed to live in harmony with other beings. This means he has to think beyond himself. While he has, no doubt, to look for himself and his family, he is duty bound to associate himself with others in the external world. He has to play a bigger role, beyond his family, in the universal family of mankind and other beings and elements of nature.

In other words, he is required to share his joy and sorrows with others in they society. As he needs help from other sources, he is also supposed to help others. One should think of larger interest of the society, the country and the nation as a whole. This will happen if we are not selfish.

It is rightly said that this world is like a big family. Therefore our self-approach has to be enlarged in the interest of the whole world. To start with, we should work in companionship with our colleagues, neighbours, street dwellers etc. and then enlarge our sphere of cooperation in the society.

77. Keep Material Possessions within Limit

Remember the saying *'Excess of everything is bad'*. Everything in excess is harmful. Human beings cherish wealth the most, but even wealth in excess is bad. It becomes the source of evils, like greed, jealousy, bad habits, fake pride etc. It also attracts thiefs and robbers etc. Most human beings want more and more and go on collecting more and more material objects, possessions etc. Sometimes we buy things that we do not need.

We need several things to live life. We need food to eat, dress to wear, house to live, some means of transport, etc. These are our basic needs. But we should not make unlimited desires our needs. A person does not feel satisfied with one car or one house or a few other material objects. He wants more and more of everything. This attitude leads to hoarding that can cause scarcity of goods and increase the cost also. In this way people block their wealth in purchasing several material objects which they may not need at all! Such wealth, otherwise, can be utilized for better purpose, for the welfare of the society. In India, we have great greed for gold which may be lying in tons, in peoples' households, in temples etc. We should not forget that such hoarding of gold attracted foreign invaders and enslaved our country. Even now, the same attitude of hoarding continues. It seems we, as a nation, have not learnt any lesson from our past history.

Human beings also develop attachment for the material objects which they possess or the excess wealth that they have amassed. This attachment brings grief when these possessions are lost. It is therefore, desirable that we should feel content with a fewer things that we really need and do not go on collecting material objects in excess. In this way, the concentration of wealth in a few hands can be avoided and the surplus wealth can be distributed among the needy poor in order to make their life better.

78. Regulate your Food Intake

'If there is anything we are serious about, it is neither religion, nor learning, but Food.'— LIN YU TANG

Food is an essential ingredient for the body and the soul. It is necessary to exist and for good health. It has considerable influence over the body and the mind. While excess of food is bad for health, intake of less food than necessary is also harmful. It is therefore necessary to regulate the intake of food.

We should properly regulate intake of our daily diet. We should neither eat in excess nor be underfed and under nourished. It is better to eat a little less than one's hunger. The intake of food depends upon several factors–age, physique, type of work done, season, time of the day etc. and of course your pocket. The most important factor is that one should eat only when one is hungry. Seasonal vegetables, fruits, pulses and milk products are very essential. It is better to be vegetarian. Food should be pure and well-cooked so that it can be easily digested.

Normally, one should have three main meals in a day. Breakfast should be sufficient so that its effect lasts till lunch which may be major meal of the day. Dinner should be light and it should be taken about two hours before going to bed. One may have a glass of warm milk before sleep. It is found useful for evacuation next morning. It is advisable to take plenty of green vegetables and fresh fruits. Occasional fasting is also good for the digestive system. Do not eat food in hurry or when angry. Eat only those foods which suit your temperament and the digestive system. One should have a balanced diet which has all the ingredients of nutrition. One should eat simple food free from intoxicants, excess of oil and spices. One must eat healthy food and should not run after taste. Remember the last advice 'Eat to live and not live to eat.'

79. Cultivate Good Company

According to a saying, "A man is known by the company he keeps." A company is as good as the people it keeps. This points towards the importance of good company. One should, therefore, be very good and careful in choosing one's company as it can have great influence upon one's, character, thoughts and actions.

It is worthwhile to have a few good companions who are trust worthy and of good character. The general useful rule is that one should make friends with those persons who are unselfish, and have good habits and positive thinking. Avoid mixing with people who have negative thinking, are greedy and selfish. A person should be watched and tested for sometime before making him a regular companion.

A company of the wise, experienced, virtuous and loving elders is good for the young. One can learn many things from learned companions who are wise and reliable. A friend in need is a friend indeed. With such friends, one should have an attitude of give and take as friendship is not a one-sided affair. Mature and trusted companions stand by you through thick and thin.

It is said 'Birds of a feather flock together.' Persons of similar habits, thinking and culture make for a good and enduring company.

80. *Avoid Harsh Speech*

"The tongue can act like a scissor for cutting the sweet knot of social relationship that links you to others."

—Anonymous

It is said that the cut made by some weapon can be healed with the passage of time, the cut made by harsh speech or words can never be healed! The ill effect of harsh words remains engraved on the surface of the mind.

Harsh words create better feelings in those to whom these are spoken. Such words create rift and enmity even among friends, relatives and companions. These also arouse negative feelings of revenge. Bitter words destroy goodwill and it is often hard to forget them.

During conversation, one should make use of sweet and pleasant words which would produce an effects of goodwill and friendliness. One should often make use of "Thank you" "May I help you" "Nice to meet you" and so on. One should keep away from places and avoid occasion, where there is likelihood of exchange of harsh speech and pinching words. It is easy to let fire but difficult to extinguish it. Some naughty persons are in the bad habit of using abusive language; their company should be avoided. One should not engage oneself with them in any exchange of conversation.

It is better to keep silent and observe restraint in the face of provocation. In some cases, it becomes necessary to reprimand others for their faults. In such cases, the same message can be conveyed in a firm voice without using harsh speech. Even a stern look can produce the desired effect. Sometime even the silence can be a best retort to a stupid person.

81. *There is always Scope for Improvement*

Life is an onward journey for learning, improvement and perfection. One should therefore always try to bring improvement in all spheres of life.

Bringing improvement in life is a natural process. After birth, an infant cries and tries to make some movement. Slowly he learns to turn on sides and move his hands and legs. Gradually he learns to sit, stand, walk and run. All these actions bring a lot of improvement in his life. From tiny todler, he grows into a young lad and then a full-fledged adult full of action and energy.

In the learning process, one has also to get guidance from different sources which include parents, teachers, books, daily experiences, the media etc. While external sources provide information and knowledge it is one's own efforts, intelligence and wisdom which actually bring improvements. One should, therefore, always keep on making personal efforts and use external aids wherever necessary.

There may be difficulties in the matter of bringing improvements. One has to exercise patience and strong determination in facing all odds. While self-efforts are very essential in the process of bringing improvements, one must also draw inspiration from God and pray for his guidance and success. This will create a feeling of self-confidence which promotes success in any venture. The process of bringing improvement may be slow, but remember the saying 'Slow and steady wins the race.'

82. *Follow the Path to Success*

Every one in this world wants success but not many achieve it. It is interesting to note what WINSTON CHURCHILL, the famous Prime Minister of U. K. said about success as follows:-

SUCCESS consists of going from failure to failure without loss of enthusiasm.

According to RIGVEDA 'Constant hard work with steadfastness are essential tools for success'. The constant practice of these qualities paves the path to success.

Some people work by fits and starts and then they complain about lack of success. One has to climb through all the steps of the ladder to go to the top. There may be failures on the way before achieving success. One is requested to march forward crossing various hurdles. This requires strong determination and hard work.

Put your heart, mind, intellect and the soul even in your small acts. This is the secret to achieve success. Act and work hard with an attitude full of self-confidence. This with improve your performance. One should always be cheerful and hopeful of success. A positive way of thinking builds up self-confidence and ensures success, sooner or later. A half-hearted approach to work will not help.

The path to success is not easy. Success like flowing water in the hills, flows through rocks and rough terrains. Only those who work with patience and determination achieve success in the long run. Remember the verse – Hard work and patience are two essential tools to achieve success.

83. *Practice Tolerance*

TOLERANCE is a great virtue that enables a person to face all odds.

In this world one has to live with other people who have different temperaments, attitudes and habits. No two persons are alive and there are always differences among individuals. These differences may arise while discussing something, living together, working together or while professing different religions and professions etc. There may be differences among members of the same family, neighbours, colleagues at work fellow travellers etc. Sometime there may arise differences among friends and relatives and so on.

The differences and disputes among friends and foes and among common people can be avoided and also sorted out by cultivating the sprit of tolerance by both sides and through mutual discussion and consultation. By practicing tolerance, harsh words, insulting remarks, fist fights, injuries and even murders can be avoided.

There are some exceptions to the general rule of observing tolerance. The use of tolerance has to be exercised up to a desirable limit. One must protest and raise voice against unjust and unsocial acts against the society. One must also fight against injustice and unlawful acts of other people. Tolerance should not be equated with weakness and inaction. Tolerance is a great power that enhances the strength of the body, the mind and the soul. Only strong people can exercise tolerance.

Tolerance should be practiced in association with all good and like-minded people on individual as well as collective basis. It will promote peace and harmony in the society.

84. Plan Whatever you Do

PLAN your work and then work your plan. **–Anonymous**

In order to gain success in life, you should first think wisely and then chalk out your plan of action for whatever you wish to do. Proper planning will make your work easy and ensure success. Haphazard way of working will take a long time to do anything and it may not always produce good result.

Suppose you have to perform a Journey, you can't. Just move out on the day of your journey without any preparation. First you have to decide on the day, buy the ticket well in time, prepare the baggage to be taken and so on. These arrangements will facilitate your travel.

Proper planning is essential in all activities of life which include education, profession, marriage, raising a family, building a house and so on. Without planning, one may face difficulties and also waste time and money and even face failure.

These days we hear of educational planning, career planning, money planning and even family planning which is so important for our family, the society and the country. That is why we have five-year-plan for the proper development of the country. In the some way, proper planning is most essential for self-development and success.

Therefore do not do things in a casual manner and plan your work in advance. Set your goal first, then make necessary preparation, your success will be assured.

85. Be Compassionate

Being compassionate means feeling of concern and pity for someone else who is in pain, distress or any other state of difficulty and helplessness. It does not mean mere lip service or uttering some words of outward sympathy. The feeling of concern has to be from the depth of heart as if one himself is actually experiencing similar pain or grief.

We human beings are children of God and are bound by universal kinship with others. We are compassionate when we learn to feel within ourselves the suffering and pain of other beings. The degree to which we are sensitive to the pain and suffering of other people, indicates our humanitarian quality and approach to life. The extent of our being humane to others in their misery, shows the strength of our character and compassion.

It is not only human beings alone to whom one should show compassion. We should be compassionate towards birds, animals, etc as well. It follows that we should not kill them for our food or otherwise. Those whom we kill for food are equally entitled to live in this world, as we human beings have the right or reason to do so.

Great spiritual leaders like Buddha, Mahavira, Dayananda, Kabir and many other saints were full of compassion to the highest degree. Christ was a great preacher of compassion. In recent times Mahatama Gandhi advocated love and non-violence. That is why all such great men are remembered with great respect and reverence by the society at large.

Be compassionate for your own sake and for others too, who deserve your sympathy.

86. *Goodness is Rewarding*

The fragrance of flowers may spread only in the direction of the wind, but the goodness of a person spreads in all directions.
—Chanakya.

It pays to be good. Most religions also teach us the same principle. This is also the essence of Karma Yoga. Good deeds bring forth good results in the present life or in the later life.

There is a saying, "As you sow, so shall you reap." If you sow wheat, you will get wheat and not barley. If you perform good deeds, the consequences will be pleasant and rewarding. However, goodness may not lead to immediate good results and sometime some people may cry out 'oh what have I got by being good? But peace and prosperity are supposed to come in the long run. There can also be hardships and sufferings in the way of those who are doing good! It may be difficult to explain such happenings as strange are the ways of God. But ultimately truth prevails over the falsehood and goodness gets its due reward.

A philosopher has said "Goodness is the only investment that never fails." Being good to others brings a sense of self-satisfaction and self-development. By being good to others you are in fact good to yourself as you get divine inspiration and encouragement in cultivating more goodness. Goodness is a great virtue and it is said that virtue has its own rewards.

Our holy scriptures tell us to be good and to do good. Holy sermons, good literature and good company encourage us to practice goodness. By spreading goodness our mind becomes free from several vices which include anger, hatred, greed and selfishness, etc.

Good people are a great asset to the society, religion and the country, besides the whole world. A really good person earns the respect of other people in due course. Billions of ordinary people have come and gone from this world but no one remembers them. But all great and good persons, like Lord Rama, Krishna, Christ, Gura Nanak, Sant Kabir and many others are still remembered with great respect and reverence.

Let goodness prevail in all the directions of the world and if that happens, sooner or later we shall then say "All is well with the world and God is in this heaven."

87. Remember Life's Goal

Life has been compared with a Journey and every Journey has a destination, a goal which one reaches at the end.

Some people think that life starts with birth and ends at death and therefore death is the destination or goal of life. But this is far from reality. The Journey of life continues even after death in another shape or form. 'Death is only a gateway to another life' says the GITA.

Our present life is only one step forward in the continuous Journey of life. Our next life depends upon the deeds done by us in the present and the earlier lives. There are several stopages in the onward Journey of life and God-realization or salvation is considered to be the final goal of life, when one is liberated from the cycle of birth and death and soul rests in peace in the company of the creator.

If we remember and wish to achieve life's goals, then we have to make strenuous efforts. In our worldly life we have to achieve different goals in different spheres, such as, education, marriage, career and so on. To achieve these goals successfully, we have to work very hard. In the same way, in order to achieve the highest goal of life we are required to work much more harder. With atmost purity of body, mind and soul and by performing good deeds and by having highest devotion and love for God, one can achieve the highest goal of life. This may be possible after several lives.

In order to achieve life's highest goal, one has to constantly keep remembering the goal and make best efforts to attain it.

88. Meditation Helps

The meaning of meditation is to think deeply, to contemplate etc. In the spiritual way of life, meditation has been glorified as the most sacred method for the worship God. It may be interesting to note that only human beings are endowed with this quality.

According to Swami Rama, a learned Indian spiritualist, meditation is a specific technique for resting the mind and attaining a state of consciousness different from the normal waking state. In this state, the mind is relaxed and inwardly awake. Meditation is the means to put the mind aside and watch, says OSHO. Every work done with a feeling of great devotion becomes meditation. That is why it is said 'Work is worship. It is a conscious effort to feel one's identity with God. Someone has said meditation is a true religion in practice. Such is the great significance of meditation.

For most people meditation is a process to make the mind silent, calm and peaceful. To start this process, one has first to acquire the ability to look within and be a silent observer of inner thoughts and thus gradually detach from them. In modern times, meditation has been accepted as an effective means to avoid stress related disorders, such as blood pressure, insomnia etc. It is helpful even in heart diseases and enhances the immune power.

In the spiritual domain, meditation is the sure means to attain success in the path of God-realisation. But this process requires constant dedicated practice. One has to learn the right technique from a real guru well versed in yogic discipline.

The practice of right meditation can bring about both material and spiritual happiness.

89. *Cultivate Inspiring Ways*

More than the words we say
It is the way we reach out
Day by day, with welcome hug,
a laugh to share,
a helping hand to show we care.
It is a comforting touch,
a gentle phrase, and encouraging smile
a word of praise.
It is the warmth, we give from the start
Love is the language of the heart.

—Anonymous.

Soft, sweet and inspiring words act as powerful medium to interact with others. An inspiring conversation can prove more beneficial and effective in mutual relationships. The following ways are useful:-

Most often we use words like I, my, mine, in our conversation. These reflect personal ego which is disliked by others. These words should be used only sparingly.

Always use the phrase 'Thank you' wherever the occasion arises. These are pleasing and winning words.

Instead of using authoritative words which sound like an order, use the words, 'Will you please.........' 'Will you mind'.......and so on.

You should try to extend a helping hand whenever the occasion demands by saying. 'May I help you. ......' 'What can I do for you....'

If you have done a wrong thing, say 'I am sorry ....' and apologize and admit your fault.

Do praise any good work done by others, without the use of flattery. This will have a pleasant effect.

If someone has done something good to you, be grateful and try to return the compliment.

Never use abusive language and express whatever you have to say in a temperate language.

Meet others with a smiling face as far as prudent.

Always keep God in mind. Remember HIM and you will never feel alone.

90. Adopt the Winning Way

'It you can win against yourself you can win the world.'

—Anonymous

In this world everyone wants to be a winner but there are more losers than winners. The reason is that most of us do not know how to win! Somebody wants to win a prize, a medal, a lottery, a match, a court case, a scholarship, a job or a sweatheart! Not many people get what they want. Let us see what we can do about it.

In order to win something one has to make efforts. A winner in any field has to work long, say for many years. Think of success in an examination, getting a job, winning an Olympic medal all these require constant hard work, daily practice, strong will and determination.

It is also difficult to be always a winner in life. Success and failure, winning and losing are the two sides of a coin. Success should never turn your head and failure should never break your heart! Both should be faced with an even mind. Any failure should be made a stepping stone to success. Failure is not for those who fall but for those who do not dare to get up after the fall!

In order to have the winning way, one should boost one self with courage and hard work and never underestimate one's efforts. To be an efficient driver one must learn to drive on long roads and in traffic jams. One should also keep in mind that a winner can never be a quitter. Remember that if you lose today, with your increased efforts, you can be a winner tomorrow. The spirit of facing the challenge lies at the heart of a winner.

In you face any challenge, the road to victory has in your thought that you are going to win. Such self-confidence paves the way to win.

91. *Find a Real Guru*

The meaning of GURU is one who leads you from darkness (ignorance) to light. In these days there is preponderance of hundreds of gurus most of whom are fake and are making money due to the ignorance of the misguided followers. If you are searching for an address in a dark street, you will surly need the help of someone who knows and leads you to the right place. In a way he becomes your guru, the guide.

In real life, one requires several gurus at different stages of life. At birth, your mother becomes your first guru, followed by your father and other elders. When you go to school and college, your teachers are your gurus. In a profession, your boss and senior colleagues are your guru. In married life, your wife / husband and even grown–up children can act in the similar way. Thus anybody who is well-qualified to guide you in some way, to help you to reach your goal can be your guru in the material world. Even a good book which tells you the truth can be a guru.

In the spiritual domain, only a god-realised person can be the real perfect guru–one who can guide you from ignorance to true knowledge. Such a guru has to be accepted in all earnestness and full faith. A genuine guru takes on the responsibility of guiding the disciple to attain the goal of life. It is very difficult to find such a real guru as he is the rarest of the rare persons. One has therefore to make considerable efforts to search for a real guru, test him and gradually establish right relationship with him. Mere blunt faith in any self-styled guru is of no avail.

A real genuine guru is essential for a spiritual seeker. In case one locates such a guru, one has to serve him with full faith and devotion in a spirit of self-surrender.

92. Play your Role Well

Every individual has to play some role as a human being. Birth is not in the hands of anyone, and God assigns this role on the basis of previous deeds (KARMA) of an individual. God expects everyone to play his role to the best of one's capacity and capability. Success and failure do not matter so long as one plays the role in all sincerity and with good intentions.

First of all, one has to play the role in the family one is born. This role may be of a son, a daughter, a father, a mother and so on. As a child or young man, one's duty is to serve and obey parents and to equip oneself with proper education for progress in life. As a professional one must do his work honestly and to the best of one's ability. In success one should rejoice and share his peace and happiness with others in the society. In failure, one should not lose heart and make more efforts to achieve better results in the future.

Human beings are representative of God on this earth. We should obey his laws and carry our duties and obligations in good faith and with a calm mind. Celebrate your life in the reality of whatever is available to you or comes your way by your efforts or as given by the providence. Face the challenges of life with patience and perseverance. Do not grumble, play your role well and spread the joy and peace among your fellow beings. In this way the inspiration and the grace of God will descend upon you.

93. Say no to Addictions

An addiction to any secure object brings you pain and does not give you any joy. **— Sri Sri Ravishankar**

Every form of addiction is bad, no matter whether the narcotics be alcohol, morphine or idealism. **—Carl Jung**

There are several sources of addiction in the society. It may be smoking, drinking, gambling, even eating certain type of food etc. One can also be addicted to indulgence in sensual and sexual pleasure. In simple words, formation of any habit which is beyond the normal limit and is harmful may be called addiction. All addictions are harmful. Thus smoking and tobacco chewing can cause cancer, drinking can lead to heart diseases, gambling can bring economic ruin, excessive indulgence in sex can ruin health and so on.

The conclusion is that we must not fall a prey to any type of addition. In order to avoid any addiction, first of all one should not make a beginning and if one has done so, one should discard it at the earliest. One becomes addicted to smoking, drinkings drugs etc. due to bad company and ignorance. One should, therefore avoid bad company and also seek the advice of elders, teachers and other learned persons before starting any addiction. These days we can get lot of useful information from books and the media. If we can make a start for an addition, we can also stop it. What one needs is proper guidance and strong determination.

The best way is to say 'No' to any sort of addiction in the very beginning.

94. Do not Underestimate Yourself

Some people have the capacity to do a lot, but they cannot do so because they underestimate their capability and suffer from some sort of inferiority complex. They feel they cannot do many things which other people can do. This is due to lack of self -nfidence and a wrong self-assessment.

All human beings, barring a few exceptions, are endowed with several physical and mental capabilities. Even many disabled persons have worked wonders in some fields where their normal counterparts have failed to perform. In order to be successful in any venture, one should first make a proper personal assessment of one's capability and then put in the best efforts. These would be thin no scope for any under estimation. It is also helpful to make use of ones natural and inborn instincts to determine ones inclination, attitude an right direction and sphere in which one can excel. One should never hesitate to take proper guidance from there who have fared better in life and are successful.

Do not feel that you are inferior in any way. Everyone has some weak and strong points. One should work with strong will and determination in the sphere of one's choice and success will not be difficult to achieve. At the same time, one should also not overestimate one's power or have a false notion that one can do anything or everything. In case of any doubt, one can seek proper guidance of any expert or experienced person in that field.

Therefore neither underestimate nor overestimate yourself. Have a fair assessment of your capability. Then make your best efforts and leave the rest to God.

95. Adopt A Role Model

Millions of people are born in this world and then they vanish after a short or long sojourn. Most of them are soon forgotten and are never remembered thereafter. However, there are a few exceptions of great men which include thinkers, philosophers, social and religious leaders, holy men, scientists and others who fall in a similar category. All such great people leave their foot prints on the sands of time. Their names remain recorded in the annals of history in golden letters.

The teaching, thoughts and incidents from the lives of such great persons inspire the later generation, even after they have disappeared from the worldly scene. They act as our heros, guides, and role-models. While an average person cannot rise to the heights which they have attained, he can at least, imbibe some qualities, some impressions from their lives and feel inspired and influenced to some extent. We can make them as our role model and live our life in a noble way.

We have a great and grand list of such great people in our history. They include Lord Rama, Sri Krishna, Lord Buddha, Guru Nanak, M. K. Gandhi, J. L. Nehru, S. C. Bose. Then we have Swami Vivekananda, Dr. Rajendra Prasad, L. B. Shastri to name only a few. We cannot be like them but we can adopt them as our role models and draw inspiration from their lives. If we do so, we can make our life better, more useful and successful.

In the present time a news item appeared in a local newspaper. This is related to the work of Mr. Sredharan who is known as Metro Man. The world famous *Time Magazine* called him an ASIAN HERO. In modern time, his lifestyle can act as a role model to the present generation. 'A day in the Metro Mans' Life', as it appeared in the newspaper is reproduced below.

4.00 AM	-	Gets up
4.30 AM	-	Pranaayaam
4.45 AM	-	Reads Bhagwad Gita
5.15 AM	-	Meditation
5.45 AM	-	Morning Tea
6.15 AM	-	Watches Spiritual talk by Swami Brahmanand on T.T.
6.45 AM	-	Yoga
8.00 AM	-	Bath
8.15 AM	-	Breakfast
9.00 AM	-	Enters Office
1.00 PM	-	Lunch with wife
2.00 PM	-	Goes to walk for an hour
3.15 PM	-	Enters Office
5.30 PM	-	Leaves Office- Takes evening walk
6.00 PM	-	Breathing Exercise
7.00 PM	-	Reads Bhagwad Gita
8.00 PM	-	Dinner with wife
8.30 PM	-	Scans news channels for headlines
9.15 PM	-	Goes to sleep

This represents the daily schedule of the present day great man who is presently working towards a mission to "Bring good values in all areas of national life and cleanse high places of corruption," as member of the advisory board of Foundation for the Restoration of National Values. The great example of the 'Metro Man' can act as a role model for the modern youth. One can make one's choice from a host of other dignatries and adopt one's role model to suit our life.

96. Four Spans of Human Life

According to VEDIC philosophy, life span of a human being of around a hundred year was divided into four spans. This division of life into four parts was known as ASHRAM SET-UP. It was designed to live life in an orderly and planned manner and each segment had a definite purpose to achieve. This was supposed to be the best way to live life. Brief details of this set-up are given below for the benefit of our readers:-

First Span : *Brahmacharya* — *Celibate Life*

The first span of life (ASHRAM) consisted of first 25 years of life and the purpose was to lay a strong foundation for the whole structure to life. Its main aim was to make a person fully fit and competent to live the next segment of married life. One is supposed to live a complete celebate life (Brahmacharya) during this period so that a person acquires good health, complete fitness, good character and proper general and professional skills and education. These values can be taught at home and in educational institutions, etc.

Second Span : *Married Life*

This is the second span of life up to 50 years or so. It constitutes the life of a householder when a person gets married, establishes a household, earns his living by entering into an appropriate profession and raises his family and performs all his other obligations and duties towards the family and the society.

Third Span : *Vanprastha*

In ancient time, a householder after completing his household duties would withdraw himself from his married life and would go to a nearby forest to live there. It may now be compared to some extent to a life of retirement from service or some other work etc. By this time the children are grown up and one is supposed to have fulfilled his domestic obligations and material desires. This is a period of withdrawal from family life and one is supposed to devote this time in the study of scriptures, meditation and some service to the society.

Sanyasa : *The Final Phase*

This is the period of life beyond 75 years of life. In this period, a person is supposed to say 'good bye' to his home and relatives etc and roam around as a Sanyasi (relinquish of the material life) and serve the society as a preacher of spirituality. This is a difficult period and not many people can opt for it now-a-days.

This is only a brief description of ashram set-up.

97. Who Am I?

If some one asks you "WHO are you?" The simple answer may be 'I am X, Y, Z'. In other words you will tell your name. I am Mohan, Sohan or Banta Singh and so on. But this is only your name, an identity. Even this name is not your own choice as it was given to you by your parents! So it is not your real self. Then you may also tell your profession - I am a doctor, a lawyer, a teacher and so on. Again, one may be a man, a woman, a son, a daughter, a father, a husband and so on. But these are all external identities and none of these can be your real self.

So the question who am I, needs a different answer. Let us examine it further. We are mainly known by our body, which is our visible identity. But this body is punishable and it vanishes at death. There is some entity in the body which makes it work, run and do all other Jobs. When this entity goes out of the body, death occurs. That entity is called soul. The body is just a vehicle for the soul. The material body and the conscious soul make our life.

The body is perishable and it vanishes at death. It is not the real self. The soul is the real self as it is eternal. The Bhagwad Gita describes the soul beautifully, as follows:-

"The soul is never born nor does it die at any time and never ceases to be. It is unborn, eternal, primeval. It is not slain when the body is slain."

This is your real self as it is everlasting. It continues forever in different shapes and forms. The body acts as its physical framework only. The soul cannot function without the body. The human birth is a special opportunity to attain freedom from the cycle of birth and death. It is only through human birth that God may be realized. We should therefore understand our true reality and its significance and thus make our best efforts to achieve the goal of life.

98. Four Objectives of Life

According to ancient Indian philosophy, a human being is supposed to achieve four main objectives in his life. These objectives (or pursuits) are briefly described below.

DHARMA

This is the first and the foremost objective or pursuit of life. Dharma is a Sanskrit word and it has no exact equivalent in English language. It is generally equated with religion but it has much wider significance. Dharma means that conduct of life which is worthy of practicing and which safeguards us from all evils. It is a comprehensive term which covers an entire range of values. It is not merely a way of worship consisting of religious rituals. In short it is a socio-ethical doctrine which when practiced in its true spirit regulates a disciplined, healthy, happy, beneficial and peaceful being in the society. It is indeed a master plan for making an ideal individual and the most beneficial and purposeful way of living. True dharma is based on genuine faith and devotion to God and practice of righteousness in real life. It does not consist of narrow, fanatic, communal and sectarian forms which are currently prevailing in the form of several traditional religions. It consists of the essential moral, social and spiritual concepts and practices which are required to be adopted in real life. It is the righteous conduct far from injustice in any form. It is the means to reform one's present life and for laying a firm foundation for the future destiny. It is a means for a human being to become a pure, pious and progressive person and a useful member of the society. It is an ideal way of living life.

ARTHA (Wealth) : Artha or the acquisition of wealth is the second most important objective of human life. But

Artha has to be based on dharma or moral values. The observance of dharma takes priority over wealth. Material wealth is very essential to live life. Money is the basis of material possessions. It is also said that knowledge is the greatest wealth. It consists of material as well as spiritual knowledge. Health is another form of wealth as the popular saying goes 'Health is wealth.' Again contentment has also been acknowledged as the greatest wealth.

As said earlier, the acquisition of Artha (or material wealth) should be based on the principles of dharma. It is therefore necessary to regulate its acquisition, possession and expenditure through a proper control based on moral values. This wealth should be earned through fair means and not by stealth, deceit, dishonest or wrong practices. The motto 'Honesty is the best policy' should be followed in all material transactions. The saying "Excess of everything is bad" should be observed. Material wealth should not lead to false pride, violence, cruelty and injustice. Wealth should be used to fulfill genuine needs and desires should be kept within reasonable limit. The principles of truth, non-greed and hard work must be practiced for the acquisition and expenditure of money. One should not be greedy and a slave of material wealth, but be a just master of it.

KAMA (Fulfillment of desires) : KAMA in a restricted sense is sexual gratification and fulfillment of mundane desires. It is born out of physical attraction and attachment. In a limited sense, Kama is the desire for the satisfaction of sensual urges in which sexual gratification occupies the prime position. On a wider scale, it includes fulfillment of other material desires also.

There is hardly anyone in the world who is free from desires. In fact, desires act as catalytic agent for actions in life. Much of the personal and worldly progress is the result of the desire to achieve, gain or discover something. But uncontrolled desires can lead to distraction. It is, therefore, utmost important to control desires and to entertain only those desires which are beneficial.

According to the GITA, lust (Kama) anger and greed are the three gateways to Hell. Kama occupies the first place as it can lead to both greed and anger. It, therefore, follows that we should keep Kama, the great monster, under proper check and at the desirable distance in order to live a useful life. Such control can be enforced through wisdom and discrimination. We should limit our desires to a minimum essential level. All desires should be restricted to the level of genuine requirement which have to be fulfilled as a matter of duty. As a general rule, all unnecessary and superfluous cravings must be discarded, as soon as they arise. The observance of principles of Dharma plays a vital role in the curbing and control of unwanted and harmful desires.

MOKSHA (Liberation) : This is the fourth objective of human life. With this, ends the state of misery and pain which are so abundant in life. The attainment of Moksha is the highest goal of life. One has to first go through and achieve first three objectives before reaching the final stage. The attainment of Moksha is extremely difficult. This may or may not be achieved in one's current span of life except in few rare cases. It is the most difficult objective which requires utmost purity within and arduous spiritual practice, constant unselfish devotion to God and an attitude of non-attachment etc. Though this objective is extremely difficult to achieve yet it is not impossible. Several rishis and yogis are believed to have achieved this objective after constant devotion and long practice.

It may he noted that all these objectives are required to be achieved within the constraints of Dharma. While Artha and Kama are necessary for human life, these have to be accommodated within the overall control of Dharma. Without the practice of Dharma, further progress and achievements are not possible. While Artha and Kama may be discarded with the passage of time as one marches forward in the journey of life, Dharma remains the constant companion till the final destination. The practice of Dharma is therefore utmost important for self-development.

99. If i Can

If I can throw a single ray of light,
Across the darkened pathway of another
If I can aid some soul to clear sight
Of light and duty and thus bless my brother
If I can wipe from any human cheek a tear
I shall not have, then, lived in vain while here.
If I can guide some erring to truth
Inspire within his heart a sense of duty,
If I can plant within the soul of a rosy plant
A sense of light, a love of truth and beauty;
If I can teach one man that God and Heaven are near,
I shall not have then lived in vain while here.
If from my mind a can banish the doubt and fear
And keep my life attuned to truth, live and kindness,
If I can scatter light and hope and cheer
And help and remove the curse of mental blindness,
If I can make joy more, more hope, less pain
I shall not have lived in vain while here.
If by life's roadside I can plant a tree
Beneath whose shade some wearied head may rest,
Though I may never share its shade or see
Its beauty I shall yet be truly blessed
Though no one knows my name.

100. *Healthy Ageing*

All things decline and decay with the passage of time. As the day passes, life follows its course of ascent and decent. Time keeps flying and age diminishes the body and decreases life. The childhood enters youth, middle-age and then old age beings.

All physical and mental faculties weaken and lose their strength with the arrival of old age. The eyesight weakens, the power of hearing is diminished, bones and muscles lose their strength, the memory diminishes, movement become difficult and the healthy body becomes a victim of several diseases and so on. In many cases old age becomes a curse!

One must, therefore, wake up, be alert and make all appropriate efforts and take necessary precautions to avoid the effects of old age. One must plan for healthy ageing. Regular physical exercise, proper timely food, healthy lifestyle, proper rest and relaxation along with good company are some of the means for healthy ageing. Besides, one should also seek the aid of the supreme power and seek his blessings through sincere prayer and meditation.

One should therefore make proper use of life span and try to achieve gradual progress towards perfection and fulfillment. The onset of ageing should act as a wakeup call for proper nutrition and other appropriate measures. Self-control is very essential towards healthy ageing. Remember the saying, 'Age is an issue of mind over matter. If you do not mind, it does not matter.'

A well-planned, mindful life-style is the key to healthy ageing.